V

SOUL MUSIC

The Pulse of
Race and Music

Candace Allen

GIBSON SQUARE

First published in 2012 by

UK   Tel: +44 (0)20 7096 1100
         Fax: +44 (0)20 7993 2214

US   Tel: +1 646 216 9813
         Fax: +1 646 216 9488
Eire   Tel: +353 (0)1 657 1057

info@gibsonsquare.com
www.gibsonsquare.com

ISBN 9 7 8 1 9 0 8 0 9 6 2 1 0 (1 9 0 8 0 9 6 2 1 7)

Printed by CPI Books

Contents

For Ames, Eddie, Laila and Rashed
of the twenty-first century

Introduction

There have been special sounds, sounds that go up and down in pleasing combinations, sounds that beat like the feeling inside your chest, that feel stronger against your hand, that you can make with your hands and feet as well, that sometimes you can feel in your feet on the floor even when they're still. These sounds are all around you. You learn to sing with these sounds and move with these sounds *jumping rope on the haphazard red brick sidewalks of Roxbury, Massachusetts, dancing around the maypole of its David A. Ellis Elementary School.* Some sounds are wider and deeper than the songs you sing and move to. They don't have words and wash about inside you like water from the sea.

You learn that all of these sounds are called music and they will enhance and sometimes dominate your life in ways that your still-organizing brain has not begun to imagine.

I am neither musician nor musicologist. I am a reasonably educated wanderer of mongrel roots, and magpie tendencies, manifesting all over an abundance of maps both geographic and intellectual. After an early childhood enthused by scientific occupations (palaeontology! ornithology! astronomy! archaeology!) and a brief interlude of wanting to be a spy — Bill Cosby of the ground-breaking television series I Spy was the smart one and Diana Rigg was the physical partner of The Avengers. With no concept of the truth of life Behind the Iron Curtain, and its lack of resident color, this desire made perfect adolescent sense — my soul gave over to a lifelong amour with the arts in most all its forms. I enjoyed and wanted to learn more about them for themselves alone but I was also very much an African-American child of my time, raised to strive for family, self and race, for whom most every act and interest carried social and political implications. There were the first moments of encounter: beauteous or divine, thought-provoking or exasperating, comforting or dull or dancing jubilee, but also always power, man in his glory saying 'I am here and with agency'; and out of that power, what effect beyond its occurrence of exhibit or duration? The images took me first: wanting to fall into pictures but not seeing myself represented in visual media, movies, television, magazines, paintings, or worse, seeing myself represented as grotesquery, wanting to know the hows and whys, wanting to correct them. Discovering Arnold Hauser's *Social History of Art* my second year at university, I wrote a paper on the social influences impacting Goya for a social relations class, having to convince the professor that I wasn't trying to fob off an art history assignment twice. Not long after I found my way to the notion of soft propaganda, via the writings of Jacques Ellul, which had a profound influence on my youthful hopes to forward the ideals of our Revolution via the communicative arts.

I pledged myself to the visual first of all then eventually found more freedom in a late exploration of the word; but music was always with me, providing a soundtrack to my inner and outer lives, rhythm to my sentences, essence to my characters, structure to my narratives. My first completed (and unsold) screenplay involved a professional Lindy-hopping dancer, aspiring to choreography in the world beyond black side dives against the transition from swing to bebop. My first novel was based on the life of female jazz trumpet-player Valaida Snow and sought to verbalize the physical and spiritual mechanics of jazz improvisation. The natures of all major characters of the at-this-writing work-in-progress second novel are informed by a music particular to my notion of who they are: one, Shostakovich string quartets, another early Ornette Coleman, another Congolese pop augmented by *Missa Luba,* and the most problematic Janus-facing between Billie Holiday and Schubert sonatas. With no organized writing tuition I felt my way to narrative structure via my (also unorganized) understanding of musical form. And an important portion of my life has been lived in music at some of its most intense and exultant incarnations during which time ecstasy, agony and curiosity have been experienced in equal measure.

I was trapped in the cliché of second novel purgatory. I was looking for a life-line and chose not to worry further the crowded field speculating on the progress of Barack Obama, whose election had been my professional focus for the entire twenty-one months of his candidacy. Rather: to meditate on music and its influence beyond itself in my own highly idiosyncratic fashion; upon Identity and my identity, on the Political and my politics starting from the premise, and my experience, of the three being inextricably linked. In a world in which Identity is the stuff of pride, pride's reverse and all manner of conflict, how much are we defined by the music identified as 'ours'. Are there consequences as well as delights in leaving one's own parish for the broad church? Is some part of oneself lost by venturing outside of the music with which one is identified? Does this matter?

I start on this quest with a consideration of my own listening history, for I've both lived through and, in my own very minor fashion, participated in sea changes in how all kinds of identities have been perceived. I'll then meander where my interests take me — I make no claim towards scientific sampling — considering what I see. Arising as it does out of a combination of memory and curiosity, the following isn't meant to be exhaustive and it won't be. My ideal sojourn would be with humility a constant companion. Humility may not always have the last word.

I can't dive. At a pool party when I was nine years old my best friend who was a far better swimmer than I encouraged me to try for the first time. I walked the length of the diving board, belly-flopped painfully and almost drowned. My swimming ability has improved greatly since then, but I've been known to stand on the side of a pool for twenty minutes or more trying to decide to take the plunge, more often than not deciding to forego. Not this time. Into the deep.

Into Cultural Nationalism
and Out of Same

A Personal Progress through the
Twentieth Century, Latter Half

1

We moved from Boston's Negro enclave of Roxbury, where I was born, to Stamford, Connecticut when I was six years old. My father was a dentist, born and raised in the Capital of the Confederacy, Richmond, Virginia, my mother a psychiatric social worker born and raised in Boston. He didn't want to practice in the South where segregation demanded that a 'C' for 'Colored' or an 'N' for 'Negro' be printed by his name in the phonebook lest some unsuspecting white person stumble into an office where a dark hand might venture into the reaches of his or, God help us, her decayed pink jaw. Though still in his early twenties he'd been offered a professorship in dentistry at the predominantly Negro Meharry Medical School in Nashville, Tennessee where some such tensions would have been avoided, but he knew that my mother wanted no parts of the South and in the insular world of the Southern black bourgeoisie what a different tale this all would have been. It was post-World War II High Time in America with a generation of young parents willing to leave the familiar, their families, their neighborhoods, their signposts, for what must be greener pastures. My parents were among a small coterie of educated young Negroes taking this spirit in an unprecedented direction, believing once impregnable, often dangerous, walls to be breachable and everything to be played for. They both thought Connecticut pretty. It was. It still is.

Stretched between Long Island's docile Sound and the New York State border, Stamford was one of Fairfield County's more urban towns. With a population of 92,000 it had a modicum of light industry and hence a more diverse citizenry than nearby bedroom communities of Darien, New Canaan, Cos Cob and Greenwich. Its downtown was a mix of second and third generation Italian and Polish immigrants, White Anglo-Saxon Protestants of impeccable bloodlines and discreet income with a generous smattering of secular Jews and a working class collection of Negroes that clustered about its railroad tracks, essentially out of sight and out of mind though constituting some 5 per cent of its population. For much of my early Stamford time I hardly ever saw them. After my sister was born we acquired a black housekeeper who was 'willing to do for colored' and brave the disdain of her peers with whom much value was invested in the comparative status of their White Ladies, but I seldom encountered Stamford Negroes in any number. There were a large number living on the more ramshackle street behind our first home that I was instructed to avoid in the traditional and cross-cultural manner that all 'nice' young children are warned to avoid the prevailing definition of riff-raff. These neighbors might have well been across the tracks as far as I was concerned. They weren't at my school nor did they attend the High Episcopal church at the end of the street that we did.

Which is not to say that my parents were guilty of the cardinal foolishness (and later sin) of considering us Caucasian. One lazy summer day when after studying my leg through the water of our new and highly coveted plastic wading pool I declared 'My skin is white!' my mother's vehement even angry reply was 'Well you're not! And don't you ever forget it!' I was seven and didn't know what she was so upset about. My remark was based on simple observation. By way of what I'd later learned to be refraction, my leg looked white in the water. Usually when I made observations they were appreciated. I didn't know what any of this meant, her emotion, her rejection of a straightforward and seemingly transparent truth. Something important obviously.

The promise of education for their children, superior to the average found in America's older urban centers, was a major reason for this post-war rush to suburbia and, in its neat red brick schools with Federal-style white trim, Stamford filled this bill: its classrooms well-appointed, for the most part, its teachers, for the most part, dedicated and well-qualified. Beyond the Three R's basics of reading, 'riting and 'rithmetic, the certainties of history and the edges of the rapidly expanding horizons of science, aspiring post-WWII families desired that their children be culturally enriched, to be aware of music and art for their own sakes in part, but also because in the Leader of the Free World art appreciation was both attribute and province of its Best and Brightest leadership class. Stamford did its best to oblige. We children had music teachers and music books filled with American songs. On playgrounds it might have been centuries old nursery rhymes and sassy jump rope ditties that filled the air, but in class it was Pilgrim songs, frontier songs, Southern songs complete with old folks and darkies -- that registered no more dissonance in my psyche than it did in the freckle-faced redhead against whom I competed for best grades in our class — campfire songs, patriotic songs for every holiday. Was there so very much difference between us and the Soviet Young Pioneers with their red-knotted kerchiefs and programmed enthusiasm? Many of our songs were older, dating from the eighteenth and early nineteenth century but beyond this how contrary the cultural conditioning? How different our collective warbling to stars, stripes, country and our revered Founding Fathers from theirs to hammer and sickle, Marx and Lenin? Our banner waving o'er the land of the free and the home of the brave to their Glory to the Fatherland united and free? Little, none, but what did we know?

We were America singing and so happy to be so. Whether this exaltation was shared by my Negro brothers and sisters clustered in their out-of-sight, out-of-mind schools was something to which I gave no thought, for what joyous young child considers such things beyond their view? Even now the yawning gaps between our experiences cripple my ability to imagine. I knew none of them then and had no idea of their lives. Perhaps they could have warned me.

When Stamford schoolchildren were seven we were entrusted with black and ivory plastic recorders for which we made fabric carrying cases and learned to blow. To say that we learned to play would be closer to a downright lie than wishful thinking. The sound was shrill, very, very shrill. The following year we were asked if any family or friend played an instrument. My father only had bongo drums, but he knew a trumpet-player, a rather famous one as it happens; but of what significance Miles Davis to a hopscotch-playing eight year-old entranced by the Mickey Mouse Club's dancing, singing Mousketeers? I was asked if I wanted to play either one. What an absolutely ridiculous question! Trumpets weren't for girls and bongo drums were just stupid. I was an American suburban girl child of my time. I chose a clarinet but practiced so long and hard the first few days that my still growing front teeth pierced my upper lip and produced a bloody mess. The next week I had a flute whose upper register I abhorred, with which I continued to struggle indifferently for the next several years taking lessons for which I seldom prepared, playing in school orchestras where nothing ever sounded like music. Franz Lehar's 'Gold and Silver Waltz' was barely distinguishable from F.W. Meacham's 'American Patrol March' as we violated harmonies, wreaked havoc upon pitch, spoiled Haydn's surprise and wandered aimlessly around tempi while our parents smiled and clapped politely. All of it more Puritan duty than music, this was New England after all.

Stamford parents didn't see themselves as the Babbitts of Sinclair Lewis or their beloved town as Zenith, but in the Stamford of my experience the desire for cultural enrichment was heavily leavened with a belief that the arts — even as they might facilitate access to elite status — were only for leisure. Serious approaches to its instruction that might lead to a career or profound impact on a soul's development were not encouraged, especially in music. Post World War II suburban America rocketing into the good life with the arts as yellow mustard on its backyard-barbequed hotdogs. If you wanted more spice then New York City was right down the road, but what was done in the City stayed in the City. In Stamford the arts were anodyne. Benny Goodman lived in Stamford; for what we kids knew of him it might as well have been the moon. A small outside theatre not far from our second Stamford home was built in honor of opera singer Ezio Pinza who'd starred on Broadway as well, not obscure Broadway either but no idea who Ezio Pinza was nor had I the curiosity to find out; but I did know what real music sounded like. At home music was all around, as persistent as any motion picture score, as reflective of our place and moment.

We played records, especially on weekends. My father loved music. Back home in Richmond, his mother had belonged to the Treble Clef, a Society composed of educated Negro women of cultivated tastes who discussed literature and sponsored concerts as well as providing living accommodation for such luminaries as Paul Robeson and Marian Anderson who though often performing in its prestigious venues would not be welcome in the city's white establishments. The Treble Clef was particularly partial to operetta and the classical efforts of Negro composers; they had no truck with jazz. My father sang starring roles in Gilbert & Sullivan at his Negro undergraduate college, listened to Toscanini broadcasts on the radio and bought very cheap classical lps as a consequence, but from its initial stirrings in the early 1940s his real love was bebop and the subsequent developments in straight-ahead jazz. My mother had not been raised with music so close and had no great sympathy for jazz, but she liked songs. The entire family liked songs, but we didn't sing together. We baby-boomers were the first American generation in near total sway to recorded or otherwise mediated music. As a family we played records replete with song, children's songs on records which were often golden-yellow and boxed in elaborate sets played by my brother and me on our own little machine, the grown-up songs of jazz vocalists and Broadway original cast albums towering over them all, the soaring melodies, the comical patter, the invitations to dance! I had a head for lyrics and learned the words to every score often far before I'd any idea of what they meant.

My mother died when I was twelve and two of my most vivid memories of her involve the Broadway musical. During her last months the dining room suffused with the easing sun of a mid-summer evening. The shifting curtains are orange and yellow, the table we set together is new and Scandinavian teak. The dinner will be steak, salad, corn-on-the cob and Meredith Wilson's Music Man plays in the background: trouble and trombones in River City, Barbara Cook's pure soprano, Robert Preston's clever wit and *Sprechstimme* an able alternative to Rex Harrison's Henry Higgins. Could this be more American? And our last outing together, not two weeks before her death, was to the film version of Rodgers and Hammerstein's Flower Drum Song, the story of a young Chinese girl who finds love and happiness in coming to America. The movie's album was purchased and I played it incessantly. *A hundred million miracles / Are happening every day…*

In the early 1940's upon learning that his friend and colleague Jerome Kern had been hired to compose for a planned musical on the life of Marco Polo, Oscar Hammerstein asked what kind of music he would come up with for a story set in China about an Italian written by an Irishman. Kern's reply: 'Don't worry. It'll be good Jewish music.'

Among the ironies of first and second-generation immigrant Jews providing the soundtrack to the middle of

America's Century: that Irving Berlin who, as Israel Baline, fled Russian pogroms with his parents, honed his craft at a Bowery joint named Nigger Mike's and secularized America's highest holy days with 'White Christmas', 'The Easter Parade' and 'God Bless America'. That the glory of the so-called American Song Book was a product of Gershwins and Hammerstein and Kern and Fields and Rodgers and Lerner and Warner and Arlen and Styne and Duke and Dietz and Loesser and Bernstein and on and on. Far out-numbering the *goyim* Porters, Wilsons, Mercers, Razafs and Ellingtons. This unknown or blind-eyed by the many who would have barred these talents from dancing to their own tunes at restricted country clubs, playgrounds for WASP America's privileged elite, of which in my home county there were many; certainly unknown by the young and feckless, all-American me. But the extraordinary co-dependent alchemy between America's black and Jewish out-siders — the predilection for wails forged by parallel histories of subjugation and pain, the melancholy and wry humor, the shared musical tropes of minor keys, bent notes and glissandi, the mutual sympathies and exploitations — would fascinate me as I matured. Far beyond avocation, it became a primary fuel to my career and creative choices, as well as tantalizing much of my insatiable desire to just Know.

Mutual sympathies and exploitations. Irving Berlin, who learned ragtime from black Bowery pianist Lukie Johnson and composed all his life on the black keys of the piano, what he called 'the nigger keys that [were] right there under [his] fin-gers' and occasionally signed himself 'Cooney' in correspon-dence later becoming increasingly quick to claim that 'our pop-ular song writers are not negroes... but of pure white blood... many of Russian... ancestry.' In writing the story for the film based on his career and first international hit 'Alexander's Ragtime Band' Berlin, then a Hollywood sweetheart embrac-ing the modi operandi of that town, replaced the black coon shouter of his own invention with a WASP society rebel portrayed by Tyrone Power.

And incident. My father asks, 'Did I ever tell you about Hammy Hammerstein?' He knows that I've been exploring my musical history but we haven't discussed anything for a few months. Throughout my research for Valaida and period screenplays he'd been a vital source of crucial ephemera but there hadn't been so much need of late. He is lucid and vibrant at 84, still practicing dentistry, still playing tennis and working out at the gym, but vowed some years ago that he no longer considered himself an expert on anything. I've taken that to be a variation on the 'old man's tennis' with which he used to pulverize younger challengers in decades past, for ever more interesting tidbits have been progressing to the surface as his time goes by.

'No, you never mentioned Hammy Hammerstein. As in Hammerstein Hammerstein?' meaning Oscar.

'Of course as in Hammerstein. Oscar Hammerstein was his name but he went by Hammy. Folks said his mother had been a chorus girl at the Apollo. I used to see him at the Red Rooster in Harlem. He'd be at the bar. Always wore a homburg… He was in his fifties when I saw him in the early '50s. Always turned out with French cuffs and a striped shirt, always looking good… Looked like he'd lived.'

'Was he straight?' The elaborate masquing of a stylish homosexual could explain such a pose if pose there be.

'Yeah, he was straight though I'd say he'd stopped playing the game. Said he'd done a lot of partying downtown, in Greenwich and Newport over the years… had a ruddy complexion.'

'You're telling me…? This is huge. This is very, very big.' An exaggeration perhaps but salient, yes, and tantalizing, absolutely.

My father shrugs. 'I thought I'd told you about Hammy.'

The next day in Manhattan I ask my aunt, who in the early 1950s was dancing on Broadway and studying with Lee Strasberg at Actors Studio if she'd known about Hammy. 'Hammy? Of course. Everybody knew about Hammy.'

Deconstruction. In the last century's earlier decades the well-stocked bar, good and ample food of Harlem's Red Rooster was a magnet for that community's political, entertainment and sporting life contingents (the 'everybody' of my aunt's description). The brain- and love-child of two former Pullman Porters, the Red Rooster was not a locale for black and tan fantasies like the Cotton Club and Connie's Inn of decades past, not a tourist stop for slumming whites let alone a venue for safe cross-racial impersonation. There were indeed environments in post-emancipation Black America where points were allotted for illustrious white bloodlines, connections to Washington, Jefferson or Alexander Hamilton and their like, no matter the usual duress under which such injections were acquired, but the Rooster wasn't one of them. The Red Rooster was a place of easy pride and enjoyment within America's Negro capital. Its denizens would have been well aware of the white Hammersteins: Oscar II the renowned lyricist partner of Jerome Kern on Show Boat of Richard Rodgers on Oklahoma, South Pacific, the King and I, The Sound of Music and my treasured Flower Drum Song; and before Oscar II, his grandfather Oscar I, impresario and tobacco tycoon, builder of opera houses beginning in Harlem on the cusp of its racial turn from sleeping white suburb to burgeoning black community. An indifferent respect for both Hammersteins would have been likely but playing on their name to enhance his own in the Red Rooster would have brought Hammy nothing but derision; and in the Red Rooster Hammy was welcome not derided. When an internet search unsurprisingly turned up no traces of Hammy, I ask my father the odds that Hammy was who he said he was. In other words was he the illegitimate mixed race and therefore, in American custom and law, black relative of the lyricist? Was this marrony Negro passing for white downtown and in a variety of elite watering holes while being his own black self in Harlem, unrecorded in any official family records as so much of black history and intricacies have been unrecorded in America's official record, but acknowledged enough that his name was his name, could this man's word be taken? Was he really a 'Hammerstein' Hammerstein?

'95 per cent' was my father's reply which, with a downward adjustment of 5 or 10 per cent for mists accrued about half-century memories and his penchant for subtle playing, meshed with my thinking and all I've learned of this aspect of American history.

While Oscar II was a paragon of domestic civility, the appetites of his grandfather Oscar I were epic and legion, theatrical women being a particular delicacy. Arthur, the elder Oscar's firstborn son, also a theatrical producer and the lyricist's uncle, was also prone to romantic adventure. With or without written substantiation liaison between Oscar I — or, given the cultural tradition of naming children after grandparents rather than parents and his never having been listed as having a son, possibly more likely Arthur — and an attractive, light-complected black chorus girl, while difficult if not impossible to accept for your average Caucasian ignorant of so much that has hid in plain sight, for those of us who have lived beyond the racial veil, such a notion is no reach at all.

But why 'huge' in the context of my present undertaking? Oscar II was born in 1895. In what seemed to be his fifties when he crossed my father's path in the early 1950s there would have been little age difference between Hammy and his lyric-writing relative. Though Oscar II didn't indulge in its often rambunctious lifestyle, he was exposed to the workings of the entertainment world from early childhood and worked in theatre all his adult life. The black and white theatre worlds of that era had little overlap in public view but underneath, at the sides and around back, information, cultures and rhythms were shared, cognitively or by osmosis, *pace* the American Song Book in all aspects of its creation; and it's highly unlikely that the lyricist wouldn't have at least heard of a tar-brushed, presumptive relative living the high life and bearing his name.

In 1927 the Hammerstein/Kern production of Show Boat redirected the trajectory of American musical theatre away from operetta and loosely linked comedy sketches to the fully integrated musical play, reason enough for its place in American theatrical history, but it was also the first racially integrated musical in that blacks and whites appeared on stage and sang together albeit in separate physical areas of that stage. *Innovations, yes, but coloreds in their place.* endowing its black characters with a modicum of human dignity, beginning with its opening number 'Old Man River'. Based on Edna Ferber's 1926 novel of the same name, Show Boat concerns itself with the lives and loves of those inhabiting a travelling Mississippi theatre boat called the Cotton Blossom. Among its other firsts are its sympathetic and loving rather than comically grotesque black couple Queenie and Joe and its serious exploration of miscegenation in the character of Julie, the Blossom's mulatto chanteuse who is discovered as passing for white with the usual tragic consequences. *Hapless Julie's pitiful, selfless demise became a prime and early manifestation of the theatre and motion picture archetype of what we black folks dubbed the Sacrificial Nigger, one who proved his or her benevolent humanity by willingly paying the ultimate price to save a white person or white people. Its less drastic incarnation was the Magic Negro as played, for example, by Sidney Poitier in the likes of Lilies of the Field and To Sir, with Love. A much safer designation, but with sexuality absolutely forbidden.*

Much energy and print has been expended in subsequent decades on whether or not Show Boat should be celebrated for its breakthrough mixing of races or condemned for its 'stereotypical' depiction of blacks, the generous use of the word nigger, the clumsy attempts at Negro dialect in lyrics and dialogue, the implication that Joe might be shiftless and lazy. More recently a conversation among Jewish intellectuals has focused on Show Boat as a 'crucial instance [along with Porgy and Bess and The Jazz Singer] of the Jewish imagination cloaking itself behind a black mask… portraying the [Jewish] self as black', with a similar masquing occurring in West Side Story with the Puerto Rican outsiders standing in for Jews in the minds of its creators, Leonard Bernstein, Arthur Laurents and Jerome Robbins. *Not Stephen Sondheim. From his own testimony Sondheim, that team's youngest member, seems to have been far more caught up in his ambivalence and exhilaration at being part of the creative maelstrom that birthed West Side Story than playing angst-driven sleight-of-hand with his cultural identity.* Maybe. I can't speculate on this with any authority and I admit to never having seen Show Boat myself, permeated thematically and stylistically as it is with a period of the nineteenth century that renders me and many, if not most, African-Americans distinctly uncomfortable. *Slavery still so close, freedom so yearned for and tenuous, disrespect and violence so rampant.* However, the fact that Show Boat isn't my choice of a way to spend three hours does not equate with my condemning its creators with conscious racism, products of their time as they were, awkward in their Negro characterizations as they were.

In all of her work Edna Ferber (also Jewish) proved herself a champion of the common man, the common woman in particular, and intolerant of any kind of bigotry. The fact that many of Oscar Hammerstein's future collaborations with Richard Rodgers are concerned with cross-racial tolerance and the triumph of the human spirit in the face of personal or political tyranny is solid testimony to his innate good intentions even without the introduction of Hammy; but how might the intermingling of fates, rhythms and blood that

Hammy represents have haunted the lyricist's pen and motivated his soul? What other resonances and implications in the line 'it mus' be sumpin dat de angels done plan' in the words of grandfather Oscar's putative Julie? *Though highly unlikely that Hammy's Apollo Theater chorine mother would have been 'dat-in" and 'dez-in"* Unlike his near contemporary George Gershwin who spent many nights playing piano in Harlem and researched Porgy and Bess with a trip to Geechie South Carolina, there's no record of upright family man Oscar II cavorting on the black side but how could he not, in writing Show Boat, have felt Hammy as his shade? Even, perhaps, as amanuensis? Could not what Sondheim terms Hammerstein's monumental style and vision, as well as his frequent reference to dreams, be at least tinged by his own if indirect personal involvement in one of America's greatest and, during Hammerstein's lifetime, unaddressed contradictions?

Whether or not Hammy was who he claimed to be, his titillating existence is immensely thought-provoking and the American Song Book replete with such collisions and collusions, a fine and vibrant mongrel with lessons to impart to those who deign to notice.

2

We'd moved into North Stamford and a developer's American dream tract called Chickadee Land (later, mercifully changed to Fairfield Woods) with wooded acre plots and roads named after his children Gary and Lolly, no sidewalks and the necessity of yellow-orange school busses. It was here amidst the new-to-me nature's music of bird song, woodpecker hammering, cricket scratching and babbling brook that I shared The Music Man with my mother. Middle class, middle-century America par excellence, but I was learning that I was different from those with whom I was surrounded both at school and at home, American yes, except not completely, the how centering first and most potently around dance and thereby around music.

Not long after the tap classes generated by Mickey Mouse Club enthusiasms went with the wind, I became aware of the fact that many of my schoolmates were attending ballroom dance classes to learn the fox-trot, the waltz and the rumba for later use at grown-up dances at nightclubs and balls like you saw on tv shows and in old movies (to the tunes of the American Song Book). I wanted to go too. I wanted to dance. My parents said I couldn't. When I asked why the answer was a prime example of parental ellipsis. 'You can't because you can't'; but I'd been to Richmond, Virginia a few times by then, usually piling into the car for a quick there-and-back in little over a day. I'd learned the word segregation at the advanced age of eight or nine, had been turned out into the hot Richmond sun with my ice cream soda in a paper cup rather than sitting inside at the cool and nifty drugstore counter and been admonished by my grandfather in a department store — where I couldn't try on clothes but where a display case of shiny trinkets had caught my eye — that Confederate flag jewellery could never be pretty. The reason why we never stayed long. A stupid but seemingly omnipotent set of rules that had everything to do with my not learning the foxtrot in up-North Stamford, Connecticut, rules that the post-WWII American determination and optimism of my parents couldn't breech after all.

But who cared about the foxtrot? The few times that channel-changing paused on Lawrence Welk, both the dancers and their music looked and sounded insipid with their vapid smiles and stiff torsos and its lack of thump. Young America was bobbing to the beat, coming under the thrall of another music whose pubescent singers and concerns were a universe away from the sophistications of the Broadway musical and the American Song Book. As the oldest sibling in the splendid isolation of Gary Road, with no older cousins within shouting distance nor the interactive buzz of an urban neighborhood cluing me to alternatives, my first exposure was the warblings of the teenage stars of popular television series depicting American middle-class suburban life, and oh, didn't I want what they wanted! I acquired their records, inscribed their truths on my heart, but like their well-behaved straight hair their lily-white idylls weren't mine to have; and lest I got confused, the humiliation of standing against the wall without one invitation to dance throughout obligatory after-school dances that took place far too often was dramatic underline to the fundamental difference between sugar-coated teen dreams and my reality.

Generally popular during school and after, welcome at slumber parties and on impromptu playing fields, during these times of initial courtship training I was suddenly and persistently invisible, reappearing again as though nothing had happened when the courtship exercises were complete. Again those rules, unspoken, un-discussed, but most fortunately I wasn't the only fly in this buttermilk. Sharon was my fellow desegregator and best friend since several years before, when her mother had spotted me playing outside our downtown house, thought me a good potential friend for her daughter and tracked our family down. The fact that my brother and Sharon's younger brother meshed as well entwined our families for our lifetimes. When our family moved into North Stamford there were then two Negro families in its leafy green whiteness. Sharon also had an older brother Jackie, three years ahead of us, his father's celebrity heavy upon his shoulders, traversing this minefield of adolescence and race with no allies and opaque to me but whose record collection introduced me to another sound, one not played in my house, and into a world where I might be more welcome.

'Mother-in-Law' was the first that I remember. Jackie playing it over and over, with Sharon and me making our tentative first forays into dance on the raised section of their living room which held the stereo system. New Orleans native Ernie K-Doe's un-enunciated baritone whine with a rumbling back-up insinuating into our spines, across our shoulders and down our legs creating an irresistible urge to move feet in patterns and rock hips — however ineptly to begin with — completely other from the well-mannered yearnings of Ricky Nelson and Shelley Fabares. A man singing of an adult's irritations, despairing and funny at once with something else in his voice, a catch, a timbre, a resonance steeped in something deep, something that was permeating our Stamford existence, hanging heavy about our trees and ponds, muffling our bird song. New in its manner of projection but familiar as well, heard in my father's voice, in the voice of his father in Virginia, in the voice of Sharon's father, in the voice of Dr Martin Luther King, who'd spoken in a Stamford church some years before he was known to one and all. It was also there in the voices of the friends we finally made across the tracks as we came to know that our social place wasn't amidst the trees. There was no escaping or ignoring this thing. It was apparently the most important aspect of who we were, who I was, not that I loved books and stars, pick-up softball games, going to museums in New York City and certainly not that I was an American. Best to embrace and take it as a glory, and better that patriotic songs weren't trotted forth so often in secondary school, for I could no longer sing them without question.

Radio was our arbiter of sound, during the school year listened to mostly during the evening whilst doing homework when only New York's mainstream, that is white, stations had signals strong enough to penetrate into the sticks, and during my early adolescence this was just fine. Their circus master DJs, first Murray the K of 1010 WINS New York and later Cousin Brucie of WABC had a varied playlist that was appealing across the urban teenage board: the smooth-blending black Drifters coaxing us up onto roofs and under boardwalks and the New Jersey Italian Four Seasons featuring Frankie Valli's wild falsetto. We were dancing to a 'Quarter to Three' with finger-popping white boy Gary U.S. Bonds and standing by former Drifter Ben E. King. The sweet schoolgirl longings of the Shirelles and Crystals seemed to embody our roiling emotions far more closely than the songs our parents listened to.

On the girl side as well, the street-smart sass of the caramel Ronettes and the terrifying white girl toughness of the take-no-prisoners Shangri-Las. They were all from the City and epitomized a glamour, truth and sometime danger that was at once tailored for us and just out of reach.

We weren't thinking about their color. We were dancing wherever we could — separately of course — and taking lessons on romance. I'll put up with Bobby Rydell's white bread vamping if you cut him with Little Eva's 'Locomotion'; and then for a while there our Negro sounds were gaining. Something new was coming out of Detroit with elegant beats and more sophisticated lyrics. *Sophistication here a relative term. 'You are so wonderful/ Being near you is all that I'm living for… you make the world a little bit brighter/ My heart a little bit lighter/ You're a wonderful one…'* Not the sparkle of Andy Razaf or Lorenz Hart but superior to *'I met him on a Sunday and my heart stood still/ Da doo ron-ron-ron/ Da doo ron-ron/ Somebody told me that his name was Bill…'* Our music, Negro music. Unlike the witty ditties written for the Coasters and ballads for the Drifters by Leiber and Stoller or the lovesick plaints of the Shirelles by Carole King, another generation of gifted and primarily Jewish tunesmiths working out of the Brill Building in New York City, these were written and produced by our folk. The Miracles, the Marvelettes, the Temptations, Little Stevie Wonder, Mary Wells, Marvin Gaye; and not just out of Motown. Out of Chicago, Sam Cooke, Curtis Mayfield and the Impressions, Jerry Butler; out of Memphis Rufus Thomas and his daughter Carla. More than holding our own against the vanilla milkshake likes of Lesley Gore crying at her party, Bobby Vinton's channeling of country club exemplar Perry Como and even the Beach Boys, with their celebration of California's blondes, 'woodies' and sun-kissed waves.

The words were important. We liked and sang the words, delighted in their stories and particularization of our lives, but singing was about the upper body, the upper chest and larynx for those, both the singers and ourselves, whose unschooled efforts weren't coming from the diaphragm. The beat/the rhythm, this was the thing, what we called the thing thing, starting below, in the hips, about the groin, in the interplay of bent knee, moving feet and the ground. We didn't know any of this as African survivals. All we knew of Africa was Tarzan and ooga-booga, bug-eyed natives being ridiculed by white folks, just like the bug-eyed black American maids and stepping, fetching fools that were what we saw of ourselves on screens. We'd rather see nothing of ourselves than that mess and describing anything we did as African we generally greeted with affront. *So much to learn. So very much to learn.*

There was nothing ooga-booga about this beat, this thing that was moving on up as we were moving on up into who we were, into freedom. For movement was also part of the Movement, the marching and the testifying that declared now was the time to claim our rights, our personhood and freedom. We were dancing this freedom as well, with our Wobble and our Jerk, our Boston Monkey and DC Bop, our Playboy and our Slow Drag. In the humid closeness of basements lit by minute blue or red bulbs, with our straightened hair going back to nature, we told stories as we danced. We flirted, admonished, collectively stomped and shouted, declaring our exaltation in being who we were: colored, spades, spooks, boots, niggas, folk.

3

'You don't have to live next to me
Just give me my equality!'
Nina Simone, 'Mississippi Goddam'

I've no idea what the parties of my white friends were like for we never spoke of our weekends, an unmentioned line we never crossed as impermeable and rigid as the division between us we never questioned. Us and them. Separation enforced by tradition and indoctrination. Not by law as in the South with signs announcing separate waiting rooms and drinking fountains, but equally insidious, equally determinant. I saw them in action at the year's end class dances which I often designed and so attended — with much searching up and down the Northeast Corridor between Boston and Washington, D.C. for a possible escort of good Negro bourgeois descent — and do know that gays and disco hadn't yet liberated white hips nor coordinated their movements, so the dancing couldn't have been as compelling. I do know that they were digging much of our music, until the Beatles came.

Where did our love go? Where did our music go? Where did my (white) friends go? The last as first: my white friends and I were smart girls with conventional post-mid-century teenage concerns about school and boys, but priding ourselves on our reasoned observation — such as early teenage girls can be reasoned — and our intelligent analysis. Suddenly these girls were hysterically and endlessly weeping over records and pictures throughout phone conversations, calling the Plaza Hotel in repeated frenzy during the Beatles' first New York visit. Why? When I first heard 'I Want to Hold Your Hand' on the radio I thought 'What is this noise?' We Negroes — *such an inelegant word, such an awkward, half-stepping, interim attempt at dignity in a word, but the one we used at the time and reflective in what we were between what we'd been and what we were about to become* — we Negroes, liked singers who could sing. Bel canto in its most fundamental incarnation of 'beautiful singing' would have been the term if we'd known it. The Beatles could barely carry a tune. Their beat was simplistic which was just as well because their most sophisticated movements, as far as I could see, involved flipping their hair from side to side. When we saw our heart throbs in person at the Apollo Theater in Harlem, we didn't scream hysterically; we wanted to hear them, to move with their grooves.

What was this reaction? Unfulfilled self-regard? Untapped sexual energy? Epidemic insanity? These white girls apparently thought this screaming was fun, even necessary, proof positive of the difference between us and them. Races apart. Races irremediably apart? Most of our singers weren't instrumentalists, but they had back-up bands that laid it down with bravura. If you had an instrument in your hands you should be able to play, not just strum and bang. What was this noise?

And the radio stations kept playing it and playing it, playing the other Brits as they crossed the water as well, the Rolling Stones, Gerry and the Pacemakers, the Animals, the Dave Clark Five. Playing them so much that our music started losing its place in the line-ups just as it was developing an incredible richness. Motown artists hung in there for the most part because founder and owner Berry Gordy had a most particular plan of seducing the mainstream audience via clean-cut, immaculately garbed, 'sophisticated' artistry (for the girl groups, expressions as pert and firmly tucked under as their buttocks, for the guys hips moving but never thrusting), but Wilson Pickett at his best after the midnight hour, Sam and

Dave beyond 'Soul Man', even the smooth crooning of Jerry Butler? We almost never heard them on the white stations anymore, not to mention the comic Contours (*First I look at the purse!*), James Brown, Brenda and the Tabulations whose 'dry your eyes' plaint combined with the line 'Mother's gotta go now' seemed to fully embody my teenage reality. The cooljerking Capitols and countless others who'd never had much support in the mainstream to begin with as they were too raw, too primitive, too dark in every way were now just to be found on the small black stations, which was problematic for this Connecticut de-segregator.

Integrationist I may have still been, but for all the sentiment and work towards black and white together, the answer of which was blowing in the wind, I simply could not abide the music now dominating the emotions, indeed total consciousness, of the majority of the white kids I knew, or thought I knew. With New York's black radio stations either sunrise/sunset or without the signal strength to puncture suburban skies at night, CKLW of Windsor, Ontario, across a great lake from Detroit 'the blackest white station in America' became my beacon of sanity and get-down. All this coupled with the indignity of the Beatles covering the Isley Brothers' 'Twist and Shout' and the Miracles' 'You Really Got a Hold on Me' and folks acting like they had invented not re-invented the wheel? Stole our place and our stuff, like it was just theirs for the taking, like they'd taken our forefathers, like they'd taken our work, like they'd been careless with our dreams. Same as it ever was and we didn't approve. I didn't approve. My outlook on racial politics hadn't yet changed but this music caused my eyes to shut and my jaws to clench. I could go to school where my parents' pleased but my music was across that line over which I had so little control. Them and us.

Behind this, of course, the particular American mix of

money, power, race and sex. Until the establishment of the
Public Broadcasting System and consequently National Public
Radio in 1970, all U.S. radio was commercial, i.e. dependent
upon advertisers for its income. All it put out over the airways,
music live and recorded, drama, local announcements, ser-
mons, news, was in service of selling whatever was contracted.
On the local level this might be funeral parlors, farm equipment, local brands of beer and flour, shoes and clothing
stores; on the national level, soap, tires, oil products, all that
America had to sell. The task of station managers was to come
up with broadcasting that could make the most direct link
between advertisers' product and the consumers' desire/ability
to buy, often in the case of more local product, on the install-
ment plan.

From the inception of recorded music there was a division
between popular and classical mainstream i.e. white
music/market and the 'race' i.e. black music/market. From the
early 1930s some Southern advertisers might traverse this
divide and buy fifteen-minute blocks of time to promote corn-
meal, furniture stores and pork products usually with in-house
performance by local musicians, but much of the targeted race
audience was without electricity and/or radios. With various
levels of poverty being the norm for most African-Americans
in the earlier part of that century, little real effort was made to
tap into the near-non-existent recreational black dollar.
African-American blues and early jazz artists had started
recording in the 1920s, primarily for race subsidiaries of the
major white companies but for a few black-owned companies
as well. However, outside of urban centers with sizable black
populations their distribution was makeshift, Pullman Car
Porters and other travelling professionals often throwing a
quantity into their luggage or the trunks of their automobiles,
parcels being carried by family members and the friends of

friends. The musicians were travelling as well, so their efforts were being disseminated throughout the country in the way of folk with hunger and desire but few hard resources, through sharing, imitation and onward development; but it was not until the industrial demands of the 1940s wartime economy provided a decided improvement in black incomes that the notion of black-oriented radio took viable hold.

As ever, the vast majority of the station owners were white, but a market had been recognized and would be catered to, with the harder-cored 'race', then rhythm and blues, music that was deemed far too crude for the mainstream audience's refined sensibilities. There were two periods when the racial lines and markets began to blur, in the late 1930s and 1940s hey day of swing and during the late '50s early '60s moment of urban rock and roll, rhythm and blues cross-pollination. The difference between the two however is that during the swing era there was no great difference between what black artists played for their own and what went out to a wider audience. During the rock and roll, r&b moment it was almost exclusively the more 'refined' artists with sweet voices, polite lyrics and down in the groove/gutter funks kept in civilized check that were getting the play on the white stations: Sam Cooke, the Drifters, the Shirelles, Dionne Warwick and of course Motown. But even with black grooves and groins under relative control, there was displeasure from social powers that were with a sense that this was all just too dangerously close to miscegenation and other corruptions of vulnerable white youth. Despite an appetite for r&b among their mainstream audience, station owners were loathe to promote too much 'jungle music' and thus suffer both opprobrium at their country clubs and the displeasure of advertisers who didn't want their wares associated with, and thus contaminated in reputation by, Negroes. And then salvation: just as the white audience was showing an initial taste for more grit and a propensity for sepia-inflected get down, in came the Brits, great white hopes to the great white buying power.

We young listening and dancing folk of color knew none of this of course. We merely experienced the surface manifestations, that our music was losing its place just as we were becoming more determined to take our own. And so it can start. A de facto broadcast embargo on something my adolescent soul craves for joy, a de facto embargo on an essential aspect of who the forces exterior to me declare I must be and finally I celebrate, makes me question my total understanding of what America is, about who I am within America. I'm no longer able to hear myself, and I'm edged, with a beat, towards Us vs Them.

4

'To be young, gifted and black.
Oh what a lovely precious dream…'
Nina Simone

I brought my own bulky record player with me to Harvard
without asking my future roommate if she was bringing hers
because I was convinced that I couldn't trust her to put up
with my music otherwise. Despite my increasing political
awareness and growing distrust of Caucasian power structures, having grown up around white people, Pamela's whiteness wasn't a particular burden to me, especially since she was
a very nice girl. Not all of our classmates, many of whom
came from extreme privilege, were nearly so civilized. I was
one of fifteen Negro girls in our freshman class, thereby
doubling the school's enrolment of color; so there were
thirty of us in a sea of twelve hundred of them. With my
Stamford experience I wasn't intimidated by the odds, but
Stamford hadn't prepared me for people who considered us
exhibits for their personal edification, watching us in the
common showers to see what happened to our skin color. A
few girls' heads rubbed in exploration of the mystery of our
hair. This was never tried more than once. Non-violence was
no longer our guiding philosophy. The white people I'd
known had had better manners.

Cleaving to our own was a matter of sanity as much as
political awakening, that and our own process of self-educa-
tion; for most of us, having been educated in northern
schools with their overwhelmingly white teaching and admin-
istrative staffs, knew next to nothing of our history. We knew

of the Movement because we were part of its living reality, but before, beyond slavery and George Washington Carver's peanuts, nothing. As was the case in all of America's elite universities, Harvard not only had no courses catering to our hunger to know more, but much of its faculty was of the opinion — nurture that had become nature — that there was nothing to know that was worthy of the institution's sacred reputation.

Despite their collective trust in their Enlightened independence of thought, in their nurture, all the accumulated inferences of black inferiority. The marks of Cain, the images not only live on stage and murking on screen. In print and animated cartoon the grotesque caricature of flopping lips, protruding backsides and goggling eye. In Western art, the representation of subservience and willing servitude: the blackamoor torch holders 'we are here for you, master'; the available odalisques 'we are here for you, master', the attentive mammies 'how can we serve you, master?' Docile or bestial with very little in between. In music, the gutter connotations of jazz or any powerful rhythm beyond the march, rising up on screens under images of sex, drugs and nocturnal criminality. Disowned by the sanctimonious for the fouling of innocent souls.

Denigrate, Middle English from the Latin verb denigrare. De-, away, completely. Nigrare from niger, black. Away with all this Blackness! By all means available, conscious, unconscious. These combined with a lack of curiosity both smug and complacent in its nature, became nature for these institutions. And their pride. And their policy.

Harvard's professors were not against the general notion of civil rights, would be and were mortified to be so accused, but they were far more akin to Abraham Lincoln than militant abolitionist John Brown in their deepest core. They believed in blacks' rights to fundamental freedoms, but not in our intrinsic equality as human beings save for the anointed few who demonstrated both obeisance to and mastery of the canons to which they subscribed. *To wit the contemporaneous epi-*

thet 'Lincoln was just another honky.'

In years gone by the few students of color who had entered Harvard's hallowed gates had either accepted its tenets or for the sake of so precious a diploma suffered in silence, but the times they were indeed a-changing and so were we. *Pace Sam Cooke and Bob Dylan both in 1964.* A new wave. Some of us came to Cambridge already radicalized with years of adolescent political action under our belts. Others like myself moved, from the earlier Movement philosophies exemplified by the non-violence of Dr King's Southern Christian Leadership Conference (SCLC) and the Student Non-Violent Coordinating Committee (SNCC)'s sit-in and Freedom Riders incarnation, to the more militant stance of the already long-dead Malcolm and his alive inheritors Stokely Carmichael and H. Rap Brown, leaders of SNCC's Black Power second incarnation. We parsed and accepted the philosophies of the also deceased Frantz Fanon, drank deep the teachings of Pan-Africanist C.L.R. James as we became increasingly aware of America's institutional intransigence on the question of race and the details of its predilection towards violence in pursuit of Caucasian manifest destiny as opposed to the inchoate day-to-day experience of same.

Using aggressive and reasoned discourse, demonstration and occupation, during my four years in residence we changed Harvard's minds, or at least their policies. Our efforts resulted in increased enrolment and in the Department of African and African-American Studies and the W.E.B. Dubois Institute currently headed by Henry Louis Gates, Jr.; but dealing with the breadth and depth of the entitled senses of superiority, the self-righteous sanctimony, the exploitation and ignorance was a mountain to climb, a roiling charybdis to traverse. Was it active conspiracy or a complacent imperial mindset with the superiority of European civilization as default position? The speculations I offered above derive from forty years of hindsight. At the time we didn't worry about the subtleties of this question. The point was that for centuries the prevailing wisdom had judged us lesser in all respects, *save perhaps in regards to running and fucking, in reaction to the latter of which in particular, white people, particularly white men, often behaved with terror-induced aggression.* We would change this once and for all; we would establish a new lexicon which took our own beauty, resilience, and creativity as default; and for this we needed one another.

After years of the academic individualism it had taken to arrive in these vaunted halls we were subsuming ourselves to the group, to the People. *And there was only one People, Black People, African People, despite our in the main still woeful ignorance of Africa...* As we shared historical and contemporary information among ourselves, engaged our critical faculties in a revisionist reassessment of the powers that were, dared not to be the thankful-just-for-getting-through-the-door colored folks that they'd expected, on our campus and campuses throughout the country the prevailing query was 'does he/she, do you identify?' This identification was a transitive state, a commitment to revolution, the center of our being. We were experiencing the thrill of a defensive solidarity shape-shifting into the proactive, primordial essence of homo sapient behavior with identity as our warming, leaping, captivating campfire.

'I don't care what the Lord don't 'low/I'm gonna shimmy shake anyhow..'
(personal variation on the traditional)

We moved, in our political thinking, in our notions of ourselves, the purposes of our lives and with our bodies. We danced, to the increasingly raw funk of Soul, James Brown — who had been too much in my nice middle-class girl from Stamford incarnation and I continued to be that more than anything else, finding the Hardest Working Man in Show Business almost too fundamental and male. It was the brothers who played his sides at our parties but we didn't desist. In the scream, groan and length of his grooves, where everything, horns, guitars, our stomping feet, pulsating arms, our swiveling hips, were the drum, in the sweat, his, ours — we sisters no longer concerned because our hair was worn natural — communion. We danced to Joe Tex, to Otis Redding who had already died too young *so much young death*. On the softer side Donny Hathaway grooved us out of the ivy towers into 'The Ghetto' and beyond, and Isaac Hayes caressed us with Hot Buttered Soul. Aretha Franklin was our Goddess both of heartache and thump, Nina Simone our Empress, epitomizing our rage, our range of inquiry and Endeavour, our elegance. Every party ended with 'Four Women', her paean to the truths and persistence of Black womanhood. Though we took ourselves incredibly seriously we weren't against the brown bubblegum boogies of the Jackson 5 and totally enjoyed the ever-manifesting genius of Stevie Wonder; but Motown was beginning to raise our suspicions as Berry Gordy directed the label more vigorously toward the crossover goals of swish nightclubs, the Great White Dollar and a non-threatening presentation that Lawrence Welk never welcomed but Ed Sullivan certainly did. Soul was our watchword and Blackness our religion. We were defining both as we defined ourselves.

Though 45s were still party instruments, most of us were acquiring lps by any means necessary i.e. purchase, pilfering from parents or 'revolutionary' shoplifting, what we termed 'liberation'. As we matured, listening in motion, post-bebop jazz, became increasingly important, extending its language and our language, exploring the reaches of what it and we Black people could be, its notes as explicit as any words. Miles always. Herbie Hancock, Charlie Mingus. Our spiritualists

John Coltrane, Pharaoh Sanders, and Sun Ra. The African rhythms of Olatunji; the freewheeling roamings of Ornette Coleman, Archie Shepp, Cecil Taylor. Save for spontaneous singing and chanting in during demonstrations, we seldom made music ourselves. Perhaps inevitably given the tenor of the times, none of us were engaged in serious study under the auspices of the University's excellent but deeply conservative Department of Music; but listening to music, dancing to music was our progressive ritual, our release from the liminality of the belly of our beast, Harvard's great white ivied whale. It might question and even taunt us, no matter. We had found ourselves and found Africa as well.

For many of the sisters, myself included, beyond the exaltation get-down of weekend parties, African dance became an obsessive vehicle of collective and self-expression, casual lessons soon developing into a semi-professional troupe that performed throughout the areas, rehearsals often taking precedence over our academic duties. *To get inside the rhythm and ourselves, celebrating the voluptuous rounds and agilities of our bodies. Bare feet on the stage. Pelvis, brain and torso at one with the drum. Liberation from all tyrannies including those of romance and its disappointments. We identified, preparing ourselves to be righteous warriors, but in our hearts many of us also, still, lovelorn post-adolescents, treasuring Dionne Warwick's ethereal plaints when feeling fragile. Better, healthier inside the drum.*

5

On the market front it seemed that the music had totally divided. White rock musicians were giving black bluesmen a bit of their propers: B.B. King toured with the Rolling Stones and Eric Clapton recorded with Howlin' Wolf; but black audiences have never had much sentimentality towards sounds that have passed their moment. For most of us younger, upscale college-educated, mainstream aspiring Afro-Americans, country and Chicago blues were extremely pre-Revolution. All that midnight creeping, meet me in the bottom, hearse coming, shoulda quit you, blade and railroads okey-doke be-spoke the limited horizons of yesterday's news, and electric guitar pyrotechnics weren't part of our thing. Even as we doubted his 'identification' we admired Jimi Hendrix's virtuosity, but you couldn't dance to his music, not the way we did anyway.

Though a judicious amount of weed was being passed from hand to hand in our midst (by the brothers far more than the sisters) psychedelics weren't our thing either. Revolutionaries needed to be in the here and now, and we watched the jerking bodies, flopping breasts, messy hair and shaggy clothes of our young white counterparts stretching their consciousness with disdain. We judged psychedelia but another manifestation of white privilege. Once their contortions had run their course all our white peers need do before taking expected places at the tables of power was cut and comb their hair, harness their bosoms, focus their eyes. Us and them. Ours was a Manichean universe. Whose truth would we express, ours or that of the white oppressors? There were varying degrees of the take-no-prisoners-approach, but the engine was towards the destruction of white ideas, of white ways of looking at the world, the over-riding covenant that Euro-American cultural sensibility was anti-human in its basic nature.

My undergraduate thesis was entitled 'Towards a Black Aesthetic in Visual Communications', which I posited should be explored via the rhythms present in black music, to transpose these rhythmic sounds to rhythmic color and motion within frames. I was looking to contribute my own little bit to the developing Black Arts Movement and my first pass at its opening chapter was a categorical dismissal of the entire Western artistic tradition as bankrupt, dictatorial and antithetical to all grounded human values, to which my advisor's only counter was 'Isn't this a bit harsh?' I amended my approach to a discussion of Western dualism, the divisions between high and low, body and soul which I felt stemmed from a narrow definition of Christianity that would have flummoxed Christ, but I never met with my advisor again. I despised him then as a cultural imperialist flunky and even now, decades hence, harbor resentment that he didn't challenge me in a manner that would have forced my thinking more deeply, but such were the times. At the department review of my thesis, the only comment any of the professors had was that it was 'very well-written.' Did they feel themselves ill-equipped or did they just not give a damn? I felt robbed. Perhaps they did too.

Black we might have been, but we were also privileged American baby-boomers who acted as though history began with us. In championing our music, we had no idea that a number of our innovators, Will Marion Cook, Billy Strayhorn, Fats Waller, even Miles Davis had had Western classical training and initial aspirations in that direction. We knew nothing of radical political movements earlier in American let alone world history, not even those that had affected the lives of our parents. We didn't know why European refugee professors had

fear and loathing in their eyes when we shut down their classes. *We* called *them* fascist. Though we knew ourselves to be part
of an international imperative dedicated to breaking free of
the political and cultural chains of Caucasian/Western hegemony, we had no idea that we were following previously established and concurrently pervasive tropes of cultural nationalist
behavior; but to be fair such analyses came decades after and
as a direct result of our collective upheavals. We had no road
maps, no mentors.

In his book *Natasha's Dance*, published in 2002 some thirty-
five years after we of Black student revolt's second wave were
feeling our way, Orlando Figes describes the rise of a national
school of Russian arts under the fierce leadership of critic and
scholar Vladimir Stasov, who discovered and guided the composers Mussorgsky, Borodin, Rimsky-Korsakov and Glazunov,
as well as the painters Repin, Kramskoi and Vasnetsov. Stasov's
charge was to liberate Russia's art from its European, in particular French, hegemony by finding Russia's sources in
Russia's own native tradition. In design and the visual arts this
meant a return to the decorative traditions of the steppes and
oldest Muscovy. In music it was the development of a 'tonal
mutability' based on style of peasant song and a series of har-
monic devices to create a distinct Russian style and color, suc-
cessfully accomplished and now readily recognizable in the
music of Glinka, Tchaikovsky, Rimsky and Stravinsky.
However Figes relates this tonal mutability 'was not just self-
conscious but entirely invented — for none of these devices
was actually employed in Russian folk or church music'. Just as
in the late 1960s controversial African-American academic
Maulana Ron Karenga established Kwanzaa, the December
holiday dedicated to the principles of *Kawaida*, the Swahili
word for tradition, at once embraced and reviled or just
ignored by many it was intended to liberate and inspire. Just as

black musicians of many descriptions were finding defining inspiration in the rhythms and multi-faceted speech of the African drum, just as black visual artists were celebrating the colors, textures and contours of African and Africanized bodies. One might counter that fruits of Stasov's guidance have had more lasting and significant cultural impact than the fulminations of the F.B.I. informant, more-than-occasional buffoon Ron Karenga, but that is not the point. The point is that there is a common arc to these movements, mining and celebrating that which has been disrespected and dismissed by smug prevailing establishments and turning said establishments upside down, of which we knew nothing, from which we might have garnered perspective but did not, could not.

If such information had been collected and so analyzed during our period of activity, it was not being discussed in the general academic arena. Edward Said was not yet active (*pace* his *Culture and Imperialism* published in 1993). Which prompts the question, if the case were otherwise: would we have listened and taken heed? Possibly, if we had respected the source, but we were in a tremendous hurry, dedicated to a Better Future, to our People and no one else's. We championed the Martiniquan poet and co-founder of Négritude Aimé Césaire and his *Cahiers d'un retour* but didn't linger on his wisdom,

> '… *man still must overcome all the interdictions*
> *wedged in the recesses of his fervour and no race has a*
> *monopoly on beauty, on intelligence, on strength…*'

We accomplished much but we were young and self-righteous and it was hard for anyone to tell us anything.

We knew nothing of irony and would have despised it if we had, but ironies abounded. The African fabrics in which we decked ourselves were of Dutch-manufacture and Indonesian design on British-woven stuff. Our African beads generally originated in Venice. Our interests in Black music and history

were creating a bonanza for white record companies and publishing firms as they re-issued the likes of Bessie Smith and
Billie Holiday in handsome new packaging and brought long
lost texts by black writers back onto the market. We bought
eagerly with no thought of provenance. Unbeknownst to us,
the Atlantic/Muscle Shoals generator of the most soulful of
soul music, the home of Aretha, Wilson Picket, Sam and Dave,
Isaac Hayes, and many, many more was the laboratory and
money-pot child of yet another hip New York Jew, Jerry
Wexler, and Ahmet Ertegun, an affluent jazz-lover of Turkish
descent, and the band that drove all its funkiest riffs an inter-
racial mix of Southern blacks and blues-dedicated country
white boys. More power to them, for they believed in the
sound as well as the cash; but we were jejune in our opinions
and resistant to the cross-pollinating complexities of our culture.

For all our Black-only musical declarations, outside of
political gatherings many of us joined Breughel-esque quad-
rangle revels at the release of the Beatles' Abbey Road album.
Yes, the Beatles. Here Comes the Sun heralding the end of a
long, cold, snowy winter, eluding the upraised fist of our rhetoric, and among many of us sisters Laura Nyro's mordent
poetry supported by her own musical complexities were elements of value. We might have had shameful secrets, a continuing love of Barbra Streisand, never played on campus, was
mine; but Laura Nyro wasn't shameful. In the summer prior to
my senior year I travelled to Atlanta, Georgia to work in the
first Congressional campaign of SCLC-veteran and Martin
Luther King, Jr.-intimate Andrew Young and for the first time
encountered veterans of the first wave of black student
demonstrators, the ones who'd gotten beaten, dog-bitten and
jailed. Having developed in the three previous years of intensive political discussion a definite religion-is-the-opiate-of-the-

people manner of thinking, for the first time I observed the power of black church and its music to inspire and maintain real resistance to violent power. Entertain as well. *After a long day's politicking, gathered at the candidate's home for food and all kinds of sustenance. Andy doing the holy dance with both profound belief and comic exaggeration, singing 'There's a telephone in my bosom/And I call him up from my heart.' I was and am not churched but I was glad…* Though I returned north to write my polemical Aesthetic, I was beginning to question pure rhetoric and its Revolutionary purveyors.

Black rhythm within the frame and a body-blow against polemic: It is near the end of my last Harvard year. I am in the office of the Elma Lewis School of Fine Arts across the river in Boston's Roxbury district, the neighborhood of my birth. I have spent many hours here in the last two years pursuing extra-curricular study of Afro-Cuban dance, one class of which is often accompanied by the great Olatunji himself, but I'm not dancing this day. I have come to discuss points of my thesis with celebrated and politically-minded author John Oliver Killens, who shares my interests in film and its revolutionary possibilities. We are in the School's office watching a comedy of manners unfold through the widescreen format of its information window.

A reception honouring Imamu Imiri Baraka, formerly (and often presently) known as the playwright and political theorist LeRoi Jones and primary guru of both the Congress of African People and the Black Arts Movement is about to take place, but the catering fees have not been paid. African-garbed Congress staff members are pleading with the caterer to trust in the people and contribute to the struggle, but he is unmoved. At long last the Imamu arrives, lion-tail switch of power in hand. Lithesome 'African' beauties form a double welcoming line with golden palm fronds as triumphal arch. As the Great Man and his staff enter and greet, the wide-hipped, white-clad catering staff exit heavy-laden with industrial size vats and bowls of un-paid-for soul food. As they pass near shoulder-to-shoulder neither line acknowledges the other. Wide hips sway as slim hips dip and bow. Contrapuntal rhythms even in disagreement. In the face of now ritualized rhetoric down-home common sense having its say.

6

We can deal with rockets and dreams
But reality what does it mean?
Curtis Mayfield, 'Freddie's Dead'

I moved south to attend New York University's School of Film and Television. I lasted one semester of a two-year masters program before dropping out to work on the film Superfly. The shoot was chaotic, fraught with emotions, shenanigans and financial cliffhanging that would soon become familiar to me, and I'd no idea of the film's potential importance until Curtis Mayfield's recorded draft of its score arrived in the editing room where I'd chosen to observe rather than return to my classes. Mayfield's sweet falsetto and insightful lyrics set to sexy, guitar-riffing boogie and the poignant messages pervading the score became landmarks of both the genre and its era. I loved it, still do, but I was becoming disenchanted with where much of soul was going. While Movement leaders clamored on about power and the people and many of us continued in our dedication to the struggle, the way was unclear and victories seldom unmitigated. Times were tough. Drugs and despair were rampant, and white resistance was becoming more intransigent. So much to fight against, but our music was leaving this behind. With the major exceptions of Stevie Wonder and Marvin Gaye's conceptual albums, much of Black American popular music was either ceasing to tell stories or else totally focused on the self, this also epitomized in Marvin Gaye by his shift from the political message of his 1971 album What's Going On to the deification of sex in 1973's Let's Get It On.

For much of our history, African-American music hadn't been about making money; there had been none to be made. Musicians felt lucky to scrape up enough adequate coin to keep body and soul intact; a great number of them failed. Music was about expressing what couldn't be said in other ways, about survival with joy, simultaneously the most basic and profound revelations of humanity. Its makers and receivers found within it a freedom that was rare beyond its sphere; but this changed in the late 1960s, early 1970s with their exponentially increasing market possibilities. With the burgeoning production technologies of synthesizers and multiple-tracking, producers were exercising far more power than songwriters unless they were one and the same. Bel canto, sweet or gospel rough, was no longer the first priority. Human exchange was no longer a priority. The money was in aspirational lifestyle glitz, thumping machine-generated beats anchoring the relentless surge towards gimme, and black artists wanted their piece. For the most part they, their managers and recording companies believed this was only to be found in the mainstream market, where greed was good and superficial slick the stylistic leader. If soul was about the visceral expression of truth, how could this heartless, mindless and repetitive palaver be soul? What was happening to the force that had danced me to my tribe and to myself? In retrospect I surmise that my advancing years were probably a factor in my dissatisfaction, that and an ever-increasing curiosity abetted by a privileged education and a nature I was discovering to be quietly renegade in character. Whatever the reasons, these sounds were becoming very boring and no longer speaking for me.

While most of my college friends and political fellow-travelers were completing advanced professional degrees at elite institutions I committed myself to the rough and tumble of the commercial film industry. After leaving NYU I was admitted to the Assistant Directors Training Program of the Directors Guild of America. Much of the theatrical film work to be found in New York at that time was Mean Streets and/or Blaxploitation. I worked on an unimpressive example of the genre celebrating the life of a community leader/activist cum-gangster in Brooklyn and generally had a book stuck in my pocket for the down times. If its subject matter wasn't black-oriented, the leader's henchmen challenged my racial authenticity — *'Are you Paramount [Pictures] or are you you?'* — even though I had dutifully done the leader's facile political tract and demonstrated my familiarity with African dance. They demanded protection payments in their neighborhood. They were thuggish, arrogant, stupid and annoyed the hell out of me. Some five years into my commitment to the Black Arts Movement while I still subscribed to its overall notion of building a new Black nation, celebrating the glory of Blackness through Black creativity, I was beginning to chafe at its strictures.

Though the said ideal was to break down class barriers within the community so much of what was Black was defined by working class, oppressed conditions, survival mechanisms and sensibilities. Could there be only one way of being Black, listening Black, painting Black, conjuring Black? Only one true way to pure Soul? After Stamford's social apartheid I'd been ecstatic at finding my tribe at Harvard, where our joint process and assertion of identity had been acts of both communion and liberation, but it had been so much about its particular time and place. Beyond its heady, rarefied atmosphere how willing was I to submit myself to a standardized definition of what I should think and be, even if it was draped in the liberation colors of red, black and green? *The red of our blood, the black of our skins, the green of our land.* As mentioned in the introduction, cognitively my choice of a film career had been couched in a commitment to the soft propaganda principles outlined by French philosopher Jacques Ellul, whose eponymous book had greatly influenced my undergraduate thesis, using that medium in the honing of a new mythology for Afro-Americans, and a reverence for political and artistic potency of The Battle of Algiers. But below, in that chthonic personal realm, I'd been lured by the silver phantasmagoria of Ginger Rogers and Fred Astaire, of Bugsy Berkeley, of The Great Ziegfeld, the lurid Technicolor mastery of Gene Kelly, the contemporary urgencies of Bob Fosse, of music and movement to music Hollywood style. How to accommodate such schizoid preoccupations? Could one ever?

7

'How beauteous mankind is!

How many goodly [sounds] are here!

O brave new world

That has such [music] in't!'

(with humble apologies to the Bard)

I moved again, to California. We of the metropolitan Northeast held abiding suspicions about California, Los Angeles in particular, all that Beach Boy nonsense of sun and fun, Disneyland, kidney-shaped swimming pools, no seasons as we understood them and an assumed dearth of intellectual rigor. Spanish references in street and place names rather than Algonquin, Iroquois and English. La Cienaga, La Jolla, San Francisco, Los Angeles vs. Connecticut, Quinnipiac, Massachusetts, Stamford, Boston. Different rhythms on the tongue, a language romantic rather than angular, and perhaps partial causality of the more relaxed rhythms of life in the Southland? With so much space, so much easier to lay back and let the world unfold at its own pace. Challenging to a nature more than a bit tinged with the Puritan. I never felt at home there. Driving to work very early one morning, many years into my California purgatory I looked at the passing homes and wondered what I was doing in a land where house plants were twenty feet high, but oh, these expanses!

The sky and the space so open, seemingly without limit when compared to the East. The textures of the landscape, the ionization of the atmosphere, all so other. I never developed a liking for the Beach Boys, but walking the Santa Monica beaches I understood their guitar riffs and chords as a compelling evocation of surf on sand, wind emanating from a very wide sea just as later I would that see Fragonard's pink clouds in the skies above Fontainebleau, the ridges and slender cones of cypress in Renaissance portrait backgrounds, the eerie blue-violet skies of Rene Magritte were not artistic conceits but there to be seen by the unmitigated eye. Here was a Pacific rather than Atlantic orientation and so a gateway to different worlds — to Mexico, Central America, the Far East, rather than Europe and an Africa viewed through sentimental mists. Here also a different racial mélange with Asians and Latinos now in the mix and, by grace of all these new ingredients, different musics. These had to be and were regarded as blessings for one for whom discovery was god; and as primary mediator of all this difference West Coast radio which was far superior to what I'd known in the East, all that captured audience drive time perhaps.

National Public Radio had been instituted five years before my departure from New York, but though my listening had become far more oriented to the FM rather than AM band in the years since university, I was unaware of its offerings. Despite my increasing dissatisfaction with quiet storms and mack daddy persona-ed disk jockeys I'd stayed commercial. In Los Angeles, a number of college-based stations were programming not to sell product but to broaden as well as cater to the tastes of their audiences. Ironic this given the fact that Los Angeles had superseded New York as the spiritual if not business hub of America's popular music; for our beloved Motown was but one part of a trend being ridden for all its worth by such giants as Columbia under Clive Davis and Warner Brothers' various entities. Yet in the face of this onslaught, other independent voices: KLON Long Beach with wall-to-wall straight-ahead jazz, KPCC out of Pasadena College with afternoon programming centering on swing era big band; and the master spirit, the game changer for me and countless others within reach of its signal was KCRW the lodestone of modest Santa Monica College.

Under the tutelage of KCRW's musical director Tom Schnabel I was introduced to Louisiana *zydeco*, Latino rockabilly, Portuguese *fado*, Algerian *rai*, alternative (primarily white) rock, the infectious, triumph boogie and the eerie beauty of what they called the African Beat and released from the black/white dichotomy that still dominated the East. I declared my independence from music devised by the competitive maneuvering for market share and, more importantly, the notion that there was only one manifestation of soul music, only one people in possession of soul. In all of these musics you could hear the beat of the human heart, the breath of human life force expressing its truths, joy, despair, rapture, insouciance. I still loved to dance, still attended class when I could, but save for the increasingly infrequent party get down I never listened to the glitzy empty shell that had come to encompass r&b. The poetry and musical explorations of Paul Simon and Joni Mitchell were telling me stories far closer to both my inner life and my outlook on the world. My black listening was almost exclusively jazz with an increasing interest in styles and artists from decades before my time. And then there was Western classical music.

As with so many American children of my generation, my first experience with classical music was Rossini's 'William Tell Overture' in its guise as theme music for The Lone Ranger television series. We all knew it and could sing along to it with a profusion of da-da-da's and knees-up galloping through any number of rooms. The music I'd thought of as deep and wide as a very young child was also both background and featured music for many of my favorite cartoons, Bugs Bunny, Tom and Jerry, excerpts from Fantasia and an intrinsic part of their appeal. In addition to their set of encyclopedia and a copy of the photo essay entitled *The Family of Man*, most striving mid-century East Coast homes contained at least a few long-playing records of the so-called popular classics, Beethoven Symphonies 5&6. The Huntley-Brinkley evening news featured snippets of his 9th, its origin unknown to me for an embarrassing number of years, but doing its job, guiding me through the terrifying challenges of the Cuban Missile Crisis, the assassinations of JFK, RFK and Martin Luther King, Jr. There was maybe some Brahms, the 1812 Overture, a Tchaikovsky ballet or two, Peter and the Wolf and our home was no exception. I watched Leonard Bernstein's Young People's Concerts with great enthusiasm but it was his charisma that held my attention. I enjoyed the musical interludes but retained hardly anything of what he actually said. Nothing then to rigorously compete with the exuberance of the Broadway musical or the identifying boogies of r&b.

There were exceptions of course, there must always be exceptions with something as sinuous as music that operated most powerfully in the realm beyond words and thus arbitrary capture. Franck's D minor Symphony. Heard from the living room played occasionally by my father, then appropriated for my own machine. Its brooding melancholy slithering about the slender trees of our development, at one with so much of the tenor of my adolescence. A Tchaikovsky symphony had the melancholy but not this shape. I liked the shape, the fact that it didn't seem to share all the same beats of other classics I'd heard, just as I wasn't sharing the beats of so much of where I lived, delineating my atmosphere in a manner no lyrics could capture and in the triumph of its last movement: Hope. I would be busting out of these trees. Its meaning to me never discussed with my father, for music was never discussed in our house. It was just there.

I become aware of Theodor Adorno. It is near impossible to consider music seriously without doing so. His writings on the subject are considered seminal in the field. I am years out of school but retain enough academic self-respect to read his (translated) original thoughts myself, rather than passively gulp assessment processed by others, even others I respect. (I am roughly conversant but not fluent in the language.) They are dense in the German manner. I admit that I skim and in that skimming discordant impressions and opinions criss-cross my brain: The man's abject miserabilism epitomized by the statements that 'music will be better the more deeply it is able to express…the exigency of the social condition and call to change through the coded language of suffering', his comparison of 'light' music, i.e. any music exterior to the Central European classical canon, to prostitution makes me want to run out and take the A-train while partying hearty to Sly and the Family Stone; but with his analysis of the effects of radio broadcast and other forms of commercial mediation on the reception of music by their audience/customers I am in essential agreement. His citation that due to the limited dynamic and distortions of broadcast alongside the background distraction of most listening environments 'what is heard is not Beethoven 5 but merely musical information from and about Beethoven 5', is something that makes sense to me because, in hindsight, I recognize that this is how I listened.

Those of us unacquainted with inspired live performance were gleaning from our various sources of classical music, what Virgil Thomson likened to canned food, as the technology improved not without taste and some hint of structure but not the real thing. I speak only for myself in saying that I concentrated on tunes with a vague awareness that there was something more going on, which is not to say I didn't like what I was hearing, my unschooled, irreverent 'liking' total anathema to Adorno and his co-religionists, while not knowing what that more might be; but I know that my disposition was not uncommon.

The exception for me again came by way of dance. My mother opposed my studying ballet. The daughter of Jamaican immigrants who'd arrived in the States prior to World War I, she espoused the most stringent objectives of upwardly striving Negro bourgeoisie and smart girls were meant for the professions, doctoring or lawyering — the frustrated malaise voiced in Betty Friedan's *Feminine Mystique* just not part of the norm among black women, who'd always had to supplement their partners' racially skewed incomes in order that households be viable. I was entirely too enamored with this movement distraction for her liking — while other little girls went the mommy's high heels route, at six I was strapping the ribbons of my aunt Billie's pointe shoes around my ankles and miraculously did not break them — but she had no problems with my seeing ballet. Like so many middle class little girls of New York's metropolitan area, I saw my share of Nutcrackers, and from early adolescence my father determined that I go beyond Tchaikovsky's fairy stories and attendant tutus to experience the abstract elegance of the New York City Ballet. There, with George Balanchine as my guide, I came to regard Stravinsky, Hindemith and Debussy as dance music as well as Bizet, Chopin and Schumann, all of it performed with an orchestra in the pit. While I remained completely ignorant of the formalities of musical structure, through Balanchine's choreography I was absorbing it live in four compelling dimensions and once liberated from the close scrutiny of the campus dorm and the day-to-day embrace of my tribe, first in New York City and then in Los Angeles I began feeding my curiosity and growing appreciation of the music by browsing record stores and buying what struck my fancy.

I allowed no racial identification to interfere with my love of what the human body in choreographed motion could achieve and the music through which they manifested this glory. Balanchine might declare that ballet dancers had to be small-headed, flat-butted and have complexions comparable to the inside of a peach, I didn't care. I was confident enough in my knowledge that he was wrong, had seen so much evidence to the contrary in life and on stage, that I ignored this dismissive, and yes, ignorant part of his character and continued to relish what he produced. I just wanted to feel it, explore and learn it such as I could. I finally began fairly aggressive ballet training at age thirty with the quixotic notion of being on pointe at the age of thirty-five. Chronically unhappy feet are the result of that impossible hubris but so is an abiding love for Satie, whose Gymnopédies were played for each opening barre and through whom I became entranced with the space and shimmer of Les Six.

I was becoming obsessed with the human creation of beauty with less and less care for the color of the humans involved if the art was of a high enough standard. My professional life was conducted on a freelance basis and between jobs I became a ferocious if idiosyncratic autodidact of the arts, such as was possible for one still ambitious for the Hollywood definition of success, generally keeping my off-piste meanderings to myself. Occasionally upon finding a classical album laying on the floor next to my record player, a visiting black friend would challenge me with 'Why are you listening to that?' my reply to which would be, 'Did I ask you to listen to it?' In truth I felt far less glib. The state and strength of my Blackness, my cultural identification was cause of continual soul-searching. I was border-dancing — save for the brief years at Harvard, what I'd been doing all my life. Did this make me some kind of zombie creature constituted of White aspirations and consequently self-hate? I angsted, sometimes self-reproached but the process of exploration, the ecstasy of discovery, now of the worlds beyond my tribe was in the ascendant. Polemics was on its last legs.

For all my burgeoning interest in Western classical music, for which in California the University of Southern California's public radio station KUSC was easily accessed helpmate, I was never tempted to attend a live classical concert. I'd been but to one in my life, an afternoon ordeal suffered by the New York Philharmonic for area junior high school students. They appeared stiff and bored, surely wishing to be any place other than where they were for that eternity. We were unprepared and beastly: noisy, inattentive, ostentatiously bored. In Los Angeles I could cite the domination of film both as profession and avocation as my excuse during those first years beyond the Black Arts Movement. My part of the city was strictly a company town, living for and drawing breath from only the movies, with a startling lack of interest in anything beyond its concerns. I was in good part in thrall to these concerns; but this wasn't the true reason. There was a decided Otherness about classical music's world. With its solemn, tails-clad musicians devoid of human affect when they played, its solemn, often bored, bejeweled audience devoid of human affect as they listened it was as far removed from my experience and the experience of those with whom I now aligned myself — far more loosely to be sure than when at college — as that of the head-hunters of New Guinea.

In Los Angeles my 'we' had diversified. Joined primarily by pursuit of film industry success we were of various backgrounds, educations, classes and, new to me, even countries. We were not our parents, those later characterized as the Great Generation, raised during the Depression, honed during and immediately after World War II, dedicated to family and basic decencies in the main. Many of us were taking far longer to couple, settle and procreate; and instead of the worthy accoutrements previously deemed necessary for the status of

Sophistication and the upbringing of offspring well-equipped to claim their portion of the American Dream, we were far more interested in being everything guaranteed to unsettle classical music's moneyed, affectless audience: anti-establishment, raucous, casual, ambivalent, left-leaning politically aware, counter-culturally au fait. In a word, hip. Musically speaking, straight-ahead jazz and Nina Simone were always hip. The post-modernist pose of David Byrne and the Rhode Island School of Design spawned Talking Heads was hip; Paul Simon and the South African vocal group Ladysmith Black Mombasa were achingly earnest but also hip. The thumping Mexican rockabilly of Los Lobos and the intellectual Latino beat of Ruben Blades were hip. Symphony orchestras slogging through Bruckner and Brahms were decidedly not hip, so why suffer the chagrin of being in such an environment if the music was available on record? For part of our hip was possession of the best possible sound system our budgets could sustain. Adorno's misgivings about mediated music would seem to have been resolved with one technical innovation after another vastly enhancing the experience of recorded music particularly after the introduction of the compact disk (questions about digitization would come much, much later). In the face of such wonders what else could be gleaned by attending a live classical concert when after all the music was written down and immutable and the orchestras just doing a (far, far) better job in playing it than I had with 'The Gold and Silver Waltz' way back when in Stamford, Connecticut?

The error of my opinions was made flesh via an unlikely first friendship with a young conductor, who came to conduct at the Hollywood Bowl from Britain some five years into my California sojourn. We hit it off. He didn't drive and so I became his sometime chauffeur, thereby hearing orchestra rehearsals for the first time and so the human side of classical music: the human effort, exasperation and sometime laughter beneath and beyond their Other presentation, learning that there was flexibility in the music for the first time, that there were different ways of interpreting most everything that even my unschooled ear could distinguish and decide to like or dislike. In inspired performance encountering the same frisson I'd experienced with other live music I'd enjoyed, particularly jazz, of music explored, interpreted, conveyed, received, exultant energy emanating from both sides of its equation, the doer to the receiver, the receiver to the doer. There were layers here, be it the sounding of one note by a solitary instrument or a multitude of voices melding, thrusting, counter-balancing into which I could lose and then reclaim myself with more than I had when I began.

Questions: Would I have come this way if I'd not wandered? First from the conventional expectations for a smart Negro bourgeois girl and the Northeast's ivied academia into the white working-class male dominated world of the Hollywood film crew, natural adversaries to the still highly-political me, former supporters of Barry Goldwater and George Wallace, general deriders of black folk forced to work with me and I with them. For survival, learning to concentrate on what we shared rather than the opposite. 'How can you stand being around them?' the question asked by former school friends training themselves for and later engaged in public service but having neither requirement nor propensity for commune across both color and class. With whom I lost track for many a year as I learned that we shared much, these hard-working men and I, in addition to renegade senses of humor and life, our humanity most of all.

Then, with the early film earnings, by myself to Europe, the Satanic imperium of my nationalist phase (or perhaps more appropriately Lucifer? Bearer of light before being cast into darkness for his inordinate pride?) The first trip to Britain, France and Italy when I became captivated by old stones and old pictures in their canvas, plank and pigment flesh as opposed to reproduced on a mediated and easily dismissible page. Where they were without the magic of presence. Devouring it all while, reticent with strangers, I began a compulsive photographing of doors, simple and extravagantly ornate, mullioned, architraved and linteled, the magic of their presence beckoning the Alice in me towards other realities. Then three years later to Berlin, Switzerland and Austria via work on a film, learning that work could be done in another manner, a more life-admitting manner than that known to us in Hollywood and this in the former capitol of National Socialism. Filming next to a Wall, later surrounded by Alps and hearing sounds bespeaking other human experiences but, contrary to my polemic imaginings, tantamountly human nonetheless, experiencing sources of a music I would soon hear another way. Rendering me open.

Within our Revolution, the expanding truisms of travel were given little attention. It was a different time and excursion neither so easily available nor so present in the overall consciousness as it has become. The we of my university years were among the educated elite of the world and so at the very least tangentially aware of its benefits, and with better access to ways and means than many, but the vast majority of us chose to keep our attentions rigorously inward. So many on the globe denied access to a broader view of its variety and complexities by dictatorial often once 'revolutionary' regimes while so many of us denied ourselves. In that way, despite all protestations to the contrary, so very American.

For the informed person of color there is much ancillary unpleasantness to overcome in the appreciation of Western classical music. In the United States most aggressively but by no means limited to its shores, the institutions of this music have been characterized by a social elitism designed to cosset and aggrandize its anointed. Historically this has almost always been dosed with the offhanded presupposition that blacks of whatever definition as composers, audience in the house, players on the stage were unworthy, inappropriate, at the very least incongruous. Simple, pervasive prejudice stymied the possibilities for the small handful of classically-oriented black composers and performers from slavery well into the twentieth century; but also, with the advent of jazz, the jealousy of white American classical composers at the attention and respect showered on this upstart musical fluke by admired European modernists — Ravel, Stravinsky, Bartok, Hindemith, Milhaud — was an additional factor in propelling perceptions of black and/or jazz-inspired music ever further into the low-life hinterlands of its imagined beginnings. Still, now, on screens of every format, an ill-lit and forbidding nightscape, the fug of a sleazy bar, debauched and isolated despair is further delineated by saxophone wail, trumpet probe, the walk of a bass. It is always of the dark, never of the light…

Locked as they were in their own struggle for respect before America's Old World-obsessed classical establishment, unsure of from whence should come their own inspiration, American composers such as Aaron Copland included their own George Gershwin in their disdain. This jazz was a music bereft of technical, intellectual and emotional complexity, unworthy of respectable regard let alone performance in spaces conceived to celebrate Apollonian ideals, and these only in their Caucasian incarnation. This stereotypically racist trope was counter-punched in the latter part of the twentieth century by the impassioned alternative position that, on the contrary, jazz was America's Classical Music, far more so than the offerings of musicians enthralled by European references and structures rising as it did from the particular bloods, soil and circumstance of America. One dismissive dogma exchanging taunts with another.

I came to know all this in fairly comprehensive detail, but still delighted in this music, this Western classical music, confident of its enhancement of my life and defiant of those who thought me aberrational if not objectionable. I ignored this unpleasantness as I had ignored George Balanchine's credo of the perfect dancer, just as the rapture of Tristan and Isolde would eventually consign its composer's personal nastiness to the shadows. When played with passion and commitment this music could be as soulful as any I'd ever heard and my soul was dancing. The otherness of the environment persists replete with gatekeepers demanding certain forms of behavior, certain manifestations of reverence, most particularly those who in their arrogance, their ignorance as well, consider this music the only music; but as the twentieth century became the twenty-first, new voices, new sensibilities have been questioning, changing their approaches and performances even as old guards hold tight to their dictates and the mirage of their superiorities. Heads stubbornly in the sand they are loathe to admit, let alone act on, the truth that their days and ways are numbered.

I cannot point to these new voices as the reason I succumbed. Even before being aware of these new orientations I had become hooked and remain hooked, giving not one iota of care to who approved or disapproved of my ardor, including my own sometimes questioning tribal conscience to whom I counsel 'You can be Black and find revelation in the incandescent symmetries of Bach. You can be hip, if hip you need be and find joy in the embracing humanity of Papa Haydn and the slithering impressionism of Debussy.' while finding the same in Charles Mingus and Stevie Wonder, Senegalese *griot* king Baaba Maal and Billie Holiday, the scat of Betty Carter and insouciance of the Carolina Chocolate Drops; and all of it essential elements of my self. A simple notion perhaps for those with a unified, settled and supported sense of who and what they are, but an on-going and challenging project for us whom the fates have deemed must dance on and between borders often seemingly conceived at once of acrimony and air.

Entr'acte

Without a doubt my increasing appreciation of Western classical music was abetted by my being privy to the best of the best. After many years of simple friendship we were married for a while, the referred-to conductor and I, and thereby entered a world of extreme privilege and paradox, leaving the known, where music was part of life, to the new, where music was life itself. The primary privilege: access not only to this best of the best but hearing these in process and repeatedly. This was visceral luxury akin to swimming in clear and exclusive waters of amniotic temperature and, at the same time, becoming aware in my untutored fashion of nuance and idiosyncrasies often in the locales where pieces were born and/or bred. The primary paradox: that someone of my background, political and philosophical bent should have gained entry to said world at all, so much of it exquisite in sound, trappings and attitudes, so much of it near hermetically sealed and pleased that it is so.

We of the film and writing worlds worked hard and long but not the tens of thousands of hours necessary over a lifetime to acquire musical proficiency of the highest order, a dedication that could never cease so long as performance was the desire. I reveled in the fruits of this prolonged cultivation while noting that among these dedicatees a frequent consequence of such commitment was an estrangement from worlds exterior to their own. The machinations and torments of the contemporary world were seldom palpable in the lives they led and, save for some extraordinary exceptions among them, interest in such seldom more than cursory. There was a splendid monasticism about it, all more Cistercian than

Franciscan in nature, and among the devotees that came to worship an often recherché savoring of the marvels that I'd read of in Proust and Huysmans, in Castiglione *in the harsh California sunshine, between jobs, juggling time, trucks and truculence,* but never imagined I'd witness let alone be a part of first hand. Music as bibelot, as corollary in the cult of Beauty, experienced in Vienna's Golden Hall, in aristocratic medieval courtyards of Aix-en-Province, in many of the best and architecturally-arresting acoustics in the world, heady stuff for one appreciative of beauty; *I admit to having been dancing,* and sometimes taken beyond jeweled gates to momentous effect. *Beethoven's 9th Symphony performed by the Vienna Philharmonic in the infamous stone quarry of the Mauthausen concentration camp, among the soloists were a physically disabled baritone who would have been put to death and an African-American soloist whose days would have been severely numbered, among the audience survivors and families of the lost. Later the footprints of our family imprint the plush red carpets of the Hotel Imperial with quarry dust before climbing marble stairs beneath the gazes of the Emperor Franz Joseph and his beloved Sissi.*

I danced, figuratively, literally as well at more than one Viennese ball, nineteenth century survivals, waltzing and galloping in long gloves and silk taffeta skirts, sipping champagne in between on fragile party chairs, temporary excursions into the Cinderella fantasy of many a Western girl, experienced late enough to know that such as I would never have been allowed save as servant or concubine but dancing all the same. Learning new languages, wanting to share what I was learning but never becoming other than what I was, an interloper within this world's most inner sanctum. It couldn't continue indefinitely. It didn't; but the extraordinary essence of this beauty, its exploration and propagation, treasured and still mine.

Pictures at an Exhibition

(The Twenty-First Century)

'This bitter earth…'

8

'What fruit it bears…'

Clyde Otis, as sung by Dinah Washington

I hadn't thought this all the way through. It is my first time flying to Tel Aviv, to anywhere in the Middle East in point of fact. I'd wanted to avoid the expense of British Airways and the belligerence of El Al flying out of Heathrow so chose a respected budget airline flying out of a convenient regional London airport. So instead of being one of the varied group of business people, diplomats, students, academics, tourists, and transiting relatives that constitute any airline's off-season clientele I find myself on what is essentially a charter flight for a group of extremely vibrant Orthodox Jews travelling home. They are Hasidim, primarily British in origin and appear to be inter-related. All the stringent carry-on regulations particular to budget airlines seem to have been ignored for their hatboxes and baby paraphernalia. Once the seatbelt sign has been extinguished they circulate up and down the narrow aisle as though it were a village high street. I am seated on the aisle next to two young Slavic women embarked on a tour of the Holy Land. They are simply dressed with silver crucifixes about their necks. One reads their guide book reverently to the other. We do not interact. I envy my circulating companions for their obvious happiness but I am on the aisle and bumped continually with never an apology. An announcement is made that the rear of the plane will be available for prayer at 2:30pm. At 2:30 a good percentage of the men travel to the rear to shuckle in prayer with shawls, hats and books while the women, some with prayer books open, remain in their seats. I was a de-segregator in Stamford, Connecticut, and lived on the west side of Berlin before the Wall came down; I worked the trenches of the Hollywood film industry when black folks were very rare on the ground and since settling in London in the mid-1990s often been in cultural situations, performances when if I'm not the only person of brownish color about I'm one of very few; but I can't remember feeling so aggressively surrounded as I do here now, which surprises me. I am in contained fight or flight mode, my senses alert, my adrenaline surging, my breathing unsettled.

Many years back, in junior high school, I spent several weeks with James Baldwin's *Notes of a Native Son* prominently displayed on my desk, the author's intelligent and challenging eyes my first albeit muffled declaration to my classmates of 'I am who I am. Deal with it (as will I).' I was what? Fourteen years old? And now decades later, I pull a volume of poems by Palestinian poet Taha Mohammed Ali out of my backpack and place it on my drop-down table as counter-strike to the continuous buffeting and casual entitlement displayed by my fellow passengers, the poet's portrait equally intelligent, equally challenging, but it's only for show. Unexpected emotions have mangled my concentration. I'm not a stowaway here. I've bought a ticket for this flight just as they have, yet they are acting as though the entire space is theirs alone. I'd expected my flight to be but a neutral conveyance from one place to another; instead I feel myself experiencing an enlightening pre-sage of Palestinian frustration, hardly comparable to the sixty-two years since their *nakba*, their catastrophe of 1948 and the aggression of settlements but salient to my understanding of some of the dynamics involved; and for the flight's duration there is nothing for it.

Unable to read I access my iPod for a protective shell

between them and me. Music, but Shostakovich quartets
don't work, nor does a Schumann song cycle. I haven't had
the iPod long and, disliking earpieces, don't use it often so its
playlist isn't all that it might be. I select Paul Simon's Rhythm
of the Saints and am immediately soothed by Simon's con-
templative easy voice with its Brazilian settings because it is
part of who I've been. As cited before, I have been one with
this white New Yorker of Jewish descent for decades, never
finding him at all problematic for we are products of a time
in the Northeast of America when difference in religion
often meant little more than difference in hair color. I move
to Simon, message and beat, my own form of shuckling. I
feel better. Safer? As the flight continues so does my need for
rhythms of color: Los Lobos, Orchèstre Baobab. I yearn for
faster Aretha Franklin; I'll have to add her to my playlist
when I get home, but Baobab will do. No, with its combination of Afro-Cuban *son* and Senegalese *caramance* harmonies,
its mature multi-national line-up, one of whom has been a
practicing lawyer, Baobab is exactly right, is probably more
the present me than the still divine Aretha. I ponder these
notions as I continue to dance to my wall of sound and my
fellow-travelers continue to pay me no mind.

*Am I over-reacting? I want to believe so. This is just travel as well as,
the gods know, a topic and geography replete with over-reaction. While waiting for the minivan that will transport me and nine other passengers from
London, from the Ben Gurion Airport to various parts of Jerusalem I
hear an Israeli teenager speaking on his mobile to a friend. He wears contemporary dress, has a yarmulke secured to his short hair and obviously
been asked about his flight. He and I are alone as yet in the van. His reply,
'It was terrible! It was filled with penguins! They were impossible!' Funny,
harsh, adolescent, inappropriate but also for me a tiny glimpse into the
tumultuous rifts among Israelis themselves. Over-reaction? Maybe not.*

This trip is about music and its destination not Tel Aviv

but Ramallah, to spend a week observing Al Kamandjâti, a music school established in 2004 by Ramzi Abu Redwan, a Palestinian member of Jewish conductor Daniel Barenboim and the late Palestinian intellectual Edward Said's West-Eastern Divan Orchestra, two friends whose love of the Western cultural canon in its most probing and elite manifestation, particularly in regards to its music, put paid to the arbitrary accidents of birth that could have rendered them brilliant adversaries. In the past few years I've become enthralled with the phenomenon of Western classical-music-as-salvation, Western classical music as innovative, life-changing tool combating social and political ills, instilling hope, purpose and joy into situations seeming wretchedly devoid of same. I've been profoundly moved, giddily transported, even jumped for joy in response to the most extraordinary manifestations.

Of the Divan, which since 1999 has seated young Israeli and Arab musicians side by side to play miracles of the Western repertoire in the conviction that the agreement to play notes in a particular way is 'a single step forward on common ground,' that 'before a Beethoven symphony all are equal,' not a given of course in political life. To wit, that in the playing, a yield of tiny points of light, a flush of the minor miraculous, as sometimes, in spite of itself, mutual curiosity develops where formerly rote prejudice and dismissal reigned. That this is neither an easy nor straight-forward process is exemplified in Elena Cheah's excellent compendium published in 2009 *Orchestra Without Borders,* the courage of this participation made additionally resonant by the fact that the names of orchestra members have traditionally remained unnoted in concert programs when they tour.

Of the Buskaid String Ensemble, the performing arm of

the Buskaid Soweto String Project established by British violist Rosemary Narden in 1997 to give impoverished children
of that South African township an opportunity to learn classical stringed instruments 'to the highest possible standard',
whom I witnessed injecting the urgent punch of township
kwela music into the lilt of Jean-Philippe Rameau during the
Proms season of 2007. African *djembe* drums upon which the
player sits replacing timpani, string musicians doubling as
dancers integrating the polyrhythms of the *isicathulo*, the min-
ers' gumboot dance, into a contre-danse from Rameau's
opera *Les Boréades*. North with south, black with white.
Eighteenth-century court divertissement with twentieth-century protest percussion.

Of the Simón Bolivar Youth Orchestra of Venezuela, the
pinnacle of that country's Fundación Musical Simón Bolivar,
Fundamuscial or El Sistema for short, begun in 1975 by
economist and amateur musician-cum-visionary Dr José
Antonio Abreu with a few students and nine music stands in
a parking lot and now catering to near 400,000 students in
286 centers throughout a country where more children are
engaged in the serious study of music than in organized
sport, whose concerts have created world-wide sensation as
well as the conviction among some that the salvation in question will be of classical music itself.

I have been far from alone in this appreciation yet even as I
revel in the music generated by these groups, gladdened in
my heart that a music not considered the natural choice for
peoples of color is being played so well by them, perhaps
even transfigured by them, even in my privilege, something
gnaws.

The politics of my university years weren't mere flirtation.
I may have modulated my views via maturity and curiosity

but I grew up a member of a despised minority and certain modes of inquiry have been routed into my synapses. To wit: why has Western reception of these programs, these bands been so delirious? How much is pure appreciation, even gratitude and how much Western hegemonic thinking, a gloating that young people of color have abandoned their indigenous voices for the Western classical canon? Adopting the philosophy of its being the greatest, the most expressive of man's musical production? Young people, people of any age finding their path to fulfilment, enriching their lives via the arts is a primary tenet of belief in my conventionally godless soul, so why is my happiness for them and from them tinged with suspicion? *These resonances, these tropes of survival, and liberation.* A revolutionary rule of thumb from back in that day: 'Just because you're paranoid doesn't mean you're crazy.' I've publically eschewed basic tenets of multiculturalism more than once and yet that decades-old mantra is pinging about my brain. I've learned to trust its voice so can't dismiss it out of hand, better to ask questions, to go, to see, hopefully not unduly influenced by the prism and scars of my experience.

In the going I wish to learn why these young peoples have taken this gift so triumphantly to their hearts and, such as I am able, see whether they have experienced the tugs and stresses of a divergent identity, as I did. We of the Black Arts Movement were instinctively near duplicating an imperative that had taken hold nearly a century before and thousands of miles distant in Stasov's Russia. Had this pattern been broken or were these young people wrestling with the same? To begin I approach the Barenboim-Said Foundation, parent organization of the West-Eastern Divan.

If you study music in the deepest sense of the word – all the relationships, the interdependence of the notes, of the harmonies, of the rhythm, and the connection of all these elements with the speed; if you look at the essential unrepeatability of music, the fact that it is different every time because it comes in a

different moment – you learn many things about the world, about nature, about human beings and

human relations.'

Daniel Barenboim, Parallels and Paradoxes

I have the deepest respect for Daniel Barenboim, for his musicianship, his intellect and his political activism in a field where many of his colleagues prefer to remain in the seductive on so many levels and financially rewarding bubble of exploring the myriad possibilities of their art without undue intrusion by the cares and woes of the outside world and presenting the fruits of said explorations to a privileged few. My response to those who protest that Arabs and Israelis playing music together won't bring peace to the Middle East (he never claims that it can) and/or that the Divan is an unacceptable promotion of 'normalization,' i.e. acceptance of the persisting status quo of Israeli occupation, is another back-in-the-day adage: 'You're either part of the problem or part of the solution' and to my mind by standing up to extremists on both sides of the conflict and in the face of global complacencies Daniel Barenboim is very much part of the solution. I find his thoughts on attentive listening and musical structure, the give and take between dominant chords and the inner voices of opposition as metaphors, even suggestions, for conflict resolution utterly fascinating. We are not in complete agreement in all things, most particularly with what I interpret as his implication that his Music is the only form of this grace worthy of the name. *Though he has performed and conducted tango, that glory of his Argentinean homeland, for which the closest most reverent attention links the ears and the mind with compelling and seductive movement of the entire form, there is no mention of these recordings or dvds on his official website. One wonders if it is an affinity he considers off-message and therefore must remain discreet, as my appreciation of Barbra Streisand during my 'revolutionary' period was kept very close to my chest or the fact that a pre-eminent African-American public intellectual and jazz critic is loath to make known his love of Debussy widespread knowledge?*

Western classical music is a natural fit for one of Barenboim's talent, predilections and yes, cultural identity and he has done it great glory, but what of those for whom its selection by their soul's core is not so straight-forward? I wanted to speak to some Arab members of the Divan, not because I thought their personal challenges in sitting side-by-side with the titular enemy any more daunting than those of their Israeli counterparts, for both groups are contending with years of adversarial indoctrination and mis-education. I speculated that particularly in the bubbling cauldron of divergent loyalties and crossed purposes of the Middle East, to which can be added often reductive opinions of Arabic culture, here of all places and with very good reason some form of commonality with the cultural nationalist impulses of my youth might be part of the consciousness of the Divan's Arab members if not their allegiance. In preparation I read essays by Mourid Barghouti, poems by Mahmoud Darwish and Taha Mohammed Ali and found countless resonances between their analyses, protestations and songs, the demands for recognition of co-humanity and those of African-Americans as our Movement developed, in the essays of James Baldwin, in so much of our poetry particularly from the 1950s into the '70s, so while I wasn't actually wanting a common experience of tormented loyalties, it is what I expected.

I spoke with two charming and eloquent Arab members of the Divan: pianist Karim Said, a distant cousin of Edward, twenty-one years old, born in Jordan but living and studying music in London from a very early age and the Damascus native, half-Palestinian violinist Rawan Kurdi, twenty-six years old, then doing the same in Berlin. Both were concerned with

the state of music in their respective homes, for Karim that
Jordan doesn't take the arts seriously as an essential component of a healthy society, for Rawan, that she wanted to push
herself to a higher level of Western musical art than then possible in Syria, but neither feeling conflicted. When Karim
exhibited a precocious talent for music, his amateur jazz musician father determined that his son should only listen to
Western music because of the differences in its tonal system
from that of Oriental music, a principle to which Karim
adhered at the time of our speaking, but he didn't consider this
a judgment on the overall worth of Oriental music vis-à-vis
Western music rather a question of personal taste. Karim's
own interest in jazz had increased over the years even as he
became more expert and in demand as a classical pianist, with
Oscar Peterson, Art Tatum, Keith Jarrett and Chick Corea
making up a good portion of his iPod playlist. While she had
no particular affinity to Oriental classical music because she
too wasn't raised to it, Rawan who came to Western classical
music via her study of ballet had no such qualms about listening to contemporary Arab popular music. The playful romps
of Arab songbirds shared her iPod space with the soft ballads
of Norah Jones and Latin music, particularly salsa, while in her
classical studies she searched for the essence of Shostakovich
and Brahms. Both Karim and Rawan were proud and comfortable with who they are, but both were products of the
Palestinian diaspora, born of professional and fairly affluent
parents, for whom the crushing weight of occupation and disenfranchisement has not been the daily reality it has been for
those in the West Bank and Gaza. So perhaps easier for them
to be so equable in their opinions?

But then to Ramzi Aburedwan. The Divan hasn't had as
many Palestinian members as it would like, particularly from
Gaza and the West Bank where political unrest, border clo-

sures, curfews and a lack of teachers has made serious, consistent music study of any kind problematic, which makes Ramzi Aburedwan's trajectory all the more remarkable. Born and raised in the Al-Amari refugee camp Ramzi was a child stone-thrower during the first intifada, became its poster child in fact when at eight years-old a photographer captured him in the tear-streaked act, displaying the form of the particularly determined Little League baseball player he might have been in a different life in a different land, playing sports instead of cat-and-mouse with incarceration and death. He threw stones for years, plotting where and when for the most visceral impact. Settlers' cars were a favored target. Both his father and a brother were among those lost to the conflict, ample reasons then for anger without diminution, but when he was seventeen years old, a chance encounter with a musician and subsequently with the viola changed his life. After never paying music any particular mind, sharing the pervasive belief that the political struggle was far too important for such frivolity, he discovered in the sound world a form of personal liberation, both of body and soul. He applied himself hard enough that in a year he was invited to a summer music program in the United States which led to his being accepted at a French conservatory of music directly thereafter. One year later, in 1999, he became part of the first group of musicians invited to join the Divan and, as the years progressed, began playing his viola in Palestinian primary schools where he was told afterwards by teachers that some of the children were drawing him and his instrument rather than explosions and AK-47s. He resolved then and there to bring music into the lives of as many Palestinian children as he could. In a world for decades dominated by the political, that felt it couldn't spare the time and attention to re-shape a cultural landscape pulverized by the *nakba,* Aburedwan wanted to create the feeling in them that happened and continues to happen to him in the playing of music, an energy that contends with persistent anger, in his words, 'like purifying water'. In France in 2002 with the help of a few like-minded musical colleagues and friends he established Al-Kamandjâti, Arabic for The Violinist. Its first music classes in Ramallah began two years later when Ramzi was twenty-five years old.

My telephone interview with Ramzi took place in late morning, after his daily practice and before his duties at the school. While generous enough with his answers he wasn't enamored of extended mobile telephone use. I had to know more and decided the only real way was to see Al-Kamandjâti for myself.

It is night during my minivan transport from Ben Gurion Airport. There is little traffic. The motorway is well-lit, modern and smooth, but I can make out very little beyond its boundaries. My first notions of Israel were configured by the terrifying to young me 1960 film Exodus and its Academy Award winning score, the rousing chords and lyrics of which reverberated through U.S. culture for years. One year later the musical Milk and Honey was a Broadway hit. I didn't see Milk and Honey but we had the Original Broadway Cast Album and I committed its theme song's lyrics to memory. The similarities between it and those from Exodus are striking: 'This is the land where the hopes of the homeless/ and the dreams of the lost combine./ This is the land that heaven blessed/ and this lovely land is mine...' vs. 'This land is mine, God gave this land to me/ This brave and ancient land to me... If I must fight, I'll fight to make this land our own/ Until I die/ This land is mine.' 'Milk and Honey' was specialty market cultural froth but Exodus, the film and its music, as well as the novel by Leon Uris upon which it was based were as highly effective propaganda tools in the United States as 'The Star Spangled Banner'. Palestinian Arabs didn't figure on the cast album of Milk and Honey but they did in Exodus the film and were as nightmare-inducing to me and, I imagine, to many of my generation as the Wicked Witch of the West. Of course the refugee Jewish heroes of the film after all

*the horrors they had gone through during World War II should fight for this
land and win! And, after all, they were led by Paul Newman.*

Later, during my work for Andrew Young in Atlanta, Georgia, an
evening gathering that included a Jewish attorney working hard on the campaign, one of the many righteous Jews who worked diligently in the
Movement, ready to risk life and limb, sometimes giving life and limb. I can't
remember the conversation, something about the Yom Kippur War it would
seem, but his comment has been indelible: feet clamping together, head bowed
and fist thrust high in exact duplication of John Carlos and Tommie Smith
at the 1968 Olympics. He was tall like Carlos and Smith. The Olympians
had been silent but the lawyer declared 'Both sides of the Jordan!' My first
physical encounter with Zionism. I admired this man, found him both witty
and seductive and his tone was thrilling; but even then in total ignorance I was
slightly unsettled, no doubt in the self-same fashion that we more militant
blacks were unsettling to those unwilling to move at our desired speed.
However a large percentage of my white childhood friends had been Jewish. I
hadn't grown up in the ghetto, hadn't been caught up in the desperate dance
between Jewish shopkeepers and landlords and their impoverished and captive
clientele. I trusted my friends. I didn't know Arabs, had not been entranced
by Lawrence of Arabia and Peter O'Toole's turquoise eyes. How could these
unknown Others pierce my conscience and consciousness? They could not.

For decades nothing was present in the American media to counteract the
impressions made by Exodus and its like. To which was added, from the
early 1970s activities of the Black September Group onward, the bogey of
Arab Terrorism. Never prominently leavened in the States. I was aware of
no other truths until I left its shores. When I think now of those lyrics from
the film Exodus, from the happy, seemingly innocent Milk and Honey another resonance slides onto the brainpan. Of a late 1960s recording by African-
American comedian Dick Gregory speaking of the 'discovery' of America
by Europeans: 'You tell me in that history book of yours that you came to
these shores and 'discovered' a country that was already occupied. How did
you DISCOVER something that's not only owned by somebody but that's
being used at the time?' He'd gone on. I'd laughed hard and heeded his mes-

sage. How different the European wresting of the Americas from its resident populations from the Israeli conjecture of entitlement to their 'neglected' 'desert' of a homeland? To this veteran of anti-imperial cultural and political conflict, in attitude very little.

Most of the minibus passengers, Orthodox Jews from my flight, are dropped off by lovely, modern apartment complexes. It is past 9pm but there are many pedestrians about including women and children, all dressed to their beliefs. Only the secular teen remains when I disembark at a hotel in East Jerusalem. Perhaps the driver is an Israeli-Arab. I am to take a bus into Ramallah. The parking lot is desolate. I am unsure and he concerned. Perhaps the dismissive demands of my travelling companions now behind him, he is just a decent Israeli man. I walk through the scattered debris of a busy day to a small conveyance that has seen better days. Its middle-aged driver is munching a falafel sandwich, casually dressed with ragged knit cap pulled down over his ears. He gestures two youths, passengers not employees, to help with my bag. A torn flyer with a portrait of Saddam Hussein adorns his small driver's cubicle. We will wait until he decides that there are enough passengers to proceed. There is a quiet acceptance of how things are done, no conversation. I am obviously foreign but I am welcome and for the first time since take-off I begin to relax.

The Israeli West Bank Barrier looms large as we approach the Qalandia checkpoint into Ramallah but I am exhausted and don't muse on its presence, contemplate my sense memory until later, for I have lived with a wall, der Mauer, the Berlin Wall over six years in the 1980s, the psychological as well as the physical aggressions of being denied the freedom to roam with purpose or without. West Berlin was far more blessed than Ramallah in its physical plan. It had copious parks, farmland, a forest and lakes within its barriers; one could drive at reasonable speed for half an hour without being impeded by anything more than traffic lights and good sense but after six weeks cabin fever would seep into brain cells, casting a darkness about daily activities.

The Wall was everywhere: through the Mitte, through the northern farmland, across train tracks where small trees then grew between unused ties.

Connected buoys marked the delineation on the bordering lakes and no-man's-lands with watchtowers and armed guards with a history of shooting to kill. West Berliners had three roads upon which they could travel into the rest of West Germany, straight west to Hanover, north towards Hamburg, south towards Munich but first had to pass through thoroughgoing checkpoints. As a citizen of one of the occupying Western allies I had to purchase a visa at the checkpoint but in a separate facility every time we left while my partner waited in the car. On holidays of any kind the process was slowed down to snail pace just because, and could take hours. During the intense perusal of my passport I wanted to sneer 'Yes, I'm an East German attempting to escape disguised as an American Negro' but of course did not. All inconvenient and unpleasant enough for me but for my then partner, a former East German who had spent 2½ years in prison after trying to escape to West, nine months of that in solitary, the checkpoint process and the ensuing monitored passage through East Germany to the West (from which we could neither stop or deviate) were repeated exercises in rage. Holger hadn't left his home for any politics other than that of choice, the power to select what he saw, read, ate, purchased, where he could move, how he might realize his dreams, and while I knew him the decades of frustration were still very much with him. His anger was palpable and inexhaustible and he'd never been bombed. His theatrical director father while co-opted by the Party was very much alive. East Germans, Ossies, couldn't go West but the Soviet Bloc ranged far, wide and with some variety, so perhaps more a wild animal reserve patrolled by Stasi and their kin than an ever-shrinking and the most-minimally appointed cage that I will perceive Palestine to be.

I'd expected a big palaver in passing through to the West Bank, but I would learn that it's far easier to enter the West Bank than to leave. The jitney barely paused at the booth before continuing on its way, not long after stopping within easy walking distance of my hotel. The hotel was solicitous and modern, my room oddly-shaped and equipped with a loud but effective heater which I'd soon learn was not a West Bank given.

My first day. It is sunny and chill. I'd determined to visit Ramallah because I couldn't trust the newsreel-induced shorthand impressions of rubble, twisting wires, billowing smoke and anguished faces, but its reality is totally unexpected. I've spent time in Kinshasa, Nairobi, São Paolo, the Kheylitsha township of Cape Town, all places where menace, chaos and despair were palpable, and had thought to find in Ramallah a similarly charged atmosphere. At this point in time I could not be more wrong. As in Berlin the Israeli barrier isn't visible from most places in the city. It is known, it is felt and each Friday brings weekly demonstrations against its invasive arrogance and consequent requisition of ever more Palestinian land in the nearby villages of Ni'lin, Nabi Saleh and Deir Nazim, often involving stone-throwing, rubber bullets and tear gas. Just outside Ramallah's limits and seen from many vantages atop its rises, illegal Israeli settlements have come to dominate an ever-increasing number of hilltops and fields and the patrolling jeeps of the Israel Defence Force (IDF) are ever-present and assiduous, but within Ramallah the population moving to and fro in its busy streets is overwhelmingly young and committed to life. Young Ramallans are all too aware of the constrictions of space and aspirations with which they live every day yet their heads are high, their eyes open and shining. Those who are older are exhibiting more care across their shoulders, in the lines about their eyes, their tread aware of the world's insanities, but the young are devouring all sources of light allowed to permeate their cage and determined to generate more. A significant clue to what I will learn.

Searching for Al Kamandjâti in the small tangle of streets that comprise Ramallah's Old City I pass a Greek Orthodox church, various food shops and the area's mosque. Older men in kefiyas watch me without particular curiosity though I can't imagine that they see many of me about. I smell wood smoke, then hear someone practicing the drums, follow the sound and find myself before a large, purposely skewed and studded bronze door mounted amidst some very old stones. The courtyard is clean, welcoming with potted flowering shrubs, a pale-painted violin leaning against a small window niche, still and far more finished and beautiful than I'd expected. A small plaque thanks a Swedish NGO for its generosity. It is quiet in the morning before Ramallah's schools close for the day and students converge on Al Kamandjâti for their lessons. Teachers arrive at their own pace, taking advantage of the time to prepare lessons, catch up on emails and practice. They are very young to my eyes, in their early twenties up to their early thirties at most, hailing from the UK and Europe, aside from a pianist/trumpeter from the States, on modest one- or two-year contracts. Al Kamandjâti now caters to five hundred children between the ages of five and eighteen offering them access to both Western and Oriental classical music and instruments which are taken home and well cared for in the main. In addition to Ramallah, which is open for business seven days a week and often well into the evening, there are centers in Jenin and the nearby village of Deir Gessane as well as twice or three times weekly lessons offered in four surrounding refugee camps. An outpost has also been established among the refugee camps in Beirut.

The vast majority of its students are from modest backgrounds (though some affluent families bring their children across town to participate precisely for that reason) and are not multi-lingual so the teachers must combine their workload with an effort to learn Arabic. With the language barriers misunderstandings occur and progress is often slower than it might be, but the teachers' dedication to both their charges and Al Kamandjâti's overall mission is more than impressive. Slight and bearded, often with a faint quizzical smile, Ramzi himself no longer teaches. He spends the early morning playing with his infant son and making his plans for what needs to be done that day in the same manner as years before with his predetermined stone-throwing. When at the school he often sits out in the courtyard as the children arrive and congregate between lessons. They flock to his presence, particularly teenage young men, not all of them musicians, who express their appreciation of this remarkable refuge by running errands and diligently sweeping up leaves and sweets wrappings dropped by younger children. The door is open to one and all, something about which the citizens of the Old City take great pride.

For Ramzi all music is without nationality. It is simply sound. You find that which appeals and follow it, inhabit it without concern for its origin. For Ramzi Western classical music came first and Oriental second when, in order to finance his studies in France, he taught himself the *bouzouk*, the Turkish lute, and formed the Oriental performance ensemble Dal'Ouna. For others the starting point may be the opposite, with still others preferring to confine themselves to one side; but there's nothing more to be inferred by this, for in both styles the point is the liberation it produces, be it only for fleeting moments, a feeling that can be owned by nothing and no one beyond those directly involved. Ramzi is unfazed by the continuing charges of normalization swirling about Barenboim and the Divan, calmly stating that the politicians and nay-sayers have no grounds for protest against Al Kamandjâti since it teaches both Western and Oriental music. While its mission in Ramallah differs in fundamental ways from that of Al Kamandjâti: it is far more focused on developing classical musicians capable of functioning on an international level and thus assisting the entry of young Palestinians into a global conversation for which the language is music, Beethoven rather than acrimony, as opposed to introducing light into young lives too often and too soon bereft of beauty and hope, the Barenboim-Said Foundation is one of Al Kamandjâti's major contributors. The Foundation provides additional teachers as well as funds, and Barenboim himself is an attentive mentor to the Al Kamandjâti project. Funds are of course a continuing concern and, with the Palestinian Authority both short on liquidity and far too slow in its workings for so young and nimble a project, underlying support comes from NGOs in Europe and the Arab world as well as generous individuals, but not just from anyone. While USAID operates a number of programs in the West Bank and has invited Al Kamandjâti to apply for one of its grants, because of its anti-terrorism clause Ramzi shrugs off that possibility with as close as he gets to disdain with a stranger. Terrorists? Terrorism? From whose point-of-view? By whose definition? By no means has he abandoned the politics of his youth, rather he's chosen another way.

Day two. I travel with a few of the teachers in the school van to Jenin. The distance is less than forty kilometers but the length of the journey entirely dependent on how Israeli Defence Force is monitoring the roads on that particular day. There are many different kinds of roads webbing about the landscape and many of the best and most direct between two given points are prohibited for Palestinians. It will take us nearly two hours.

With its centuries-old terraces, almond trees in a filigree of white bloom, olive groves, small fertile fields surrounded by cactus and a generous scattering of red poppies the country-side is beautiful and eminently desirable. After years of near dormancy, the experiences and teaching of my most political university years are stretching their limbs, reactivating their musculature, and I am understanding why the Israelis crave and appropriate this land. I'm an American and so hail from a nation which achieved its final form via the doctrine of

Eminent Domain, theft and dominion blessed by God for his Chosen People and a possible additional reason for the decades of America's unquestioning support for the Jewish state despite the ever-more rapid turn of its government to a darker side. How does one state that has followed this template question the intent and behavior of another? Certainly not from a position of innocence. With wisdom enhanced by confessional hindsight perhaps. Not a first attribute of the United States of America, especially in this troubling period.

As we progress I find the proliferation of settlements ever more disturbing. They range between a few mobile trailers clustered behind cyclone fencing to substantial white stucco honeycombs all with distinctive red tile roofs that are easily recognizable from the air should the need for bombardment arise. Later I learn that the Palestinian custom was to embrace rather than ride the peaks with their building, thereby avoiding the worst of wind and weather. *Perhaps leaving the heights to their God?* The Israelis have taken summit after summit as their due sometimes deliberately allowing their waste and detritus to flow downwards towards the neighbors they would bid disappear. Among the more established settlements I can glimpse swimming pools. I'm told there are golf courses as well. In this land of limited water, where Palestinian olive trees are dying for its lack. I am sobered and ever more intrigued as to what approach to music is being taken under these circumstances.

We stop in Nablus to pick up a teacher of Oriental music who's a professor at the university there (Al Kamandjâti's Oriental music teachers tend to be older than their European counterparts, settled members of their communities, and all are men.). It is lunchtime and the café where we wait is filled with happily jabbering students laden with backpacks, carrying books, but what to do with all their knowledge after they're done, confined to an ever-shrinking land where little business manages to flourish? My ex-partner's frustration led him into the secret compartment beneath a car where he was eventually discovered by dogs when the car missed its ferry from Rostock. He was later bought out of prison by an uncle based in West Berlin but his rage lingered, near metastasized in fact, and what he was dealing with was mild compared to the situation facing these young people. Among young African-Americans the consequences of persistent frustration have often been urban unrest and the nihilism of gang warfare. While among these students of Nablus University I decide not to dwell on this and enjoy their infectious optimism instead. After enjoying some fresh and tasty fast food, we load back into the van and move on to Jenin.

The renovation of Al Kamandjâti's center in Jenin has also been funded by the Swedish NGO and will be dedicated a few months after my visit. Located on a narrow side street not far from the town's vibrant market, its unassuming entry climbs to two spacious floors of instruction rooms and performance space. Late one night in March 2009 a fire bomb devastated a portion of the previous Jenin facility including the room where instruments were stored. An American newspaper report that I'd discovered on the net had suggested the responsibility of Hamas, angered by Al Kamandjâti's teaching of Western classical music and of girls learning together with boys. Surely evidence of the cultural tensions I'd suspected. I gather further encouragement toward these suspicions from other contemporary reports of the arson including concern voiced by the center's director Iyad Staiti that visitors remain inside and out of view of its enemies. One year on, however, Iyad rejects both bitterness and fear saying that since the attack occurred at 4:00 in the morning, when the IDF has jurisdiction rather than Jenin's Palestinian local police there has been no investigation and he's unwilling to make speculations about

Hamas, the Israelis or anyone else. No one was hurt, he tells me. Justice could not be done, so the school immediately moved on. The instruments were replaced with funds from Palestinian President Mahmoud Abbas, the Palestinian Authority and 'international friends' in places like Qatar and the Netherlands. Lessons were moved into the courtyard while waiting for access to the present building. Prior to the arson attack the school had had eighty students aged five to sixteen. Now it had one hundred with a waiting list of scores more. An oud player who met Ramzi Aburedwan in 2002 'after the Jenin massacre' when he'd been invited to perform in France and thereafter became one of Al Kamandjâti's co-initiators, Iyad also feels no conflicting tensions between Western and Oriental music. In recreating a Palestinian cultural identity 'we are not restrictive,' he said. 'We Palestinians, we love everything nice. We love music, all music, Oriental, Western, hip hop, jazz. It doesn't matter if the Israelis like it or do it. Now we have the first orchestra ever in Jenin'. Humbled tears shot to my eyes; for during our erstwhile black student revolution, during our years of utmost commitment, we Ivy League believers spoke of our issues being a matter of life and death, but as institutionally-protected members of W.E.B. DuBois' Talented Tenth (whether we accepted this label or not) death was something we'd have had to go out of our way to experience.

I'd had my oblique brushes with violence, piling bricks as weaponry on an occupied construction site with the construction workers clamoring against the cyclone fence and baying for our blood. The bricks were heavy, their corners sharp and I realized that if one connected with my head it would really hurt; but we were escorted off of the site by state troopers before things could escalate. Later that same year I was inside a Boston community center with families celebrating the birthday of Malcolm X with game booths, music and food, when it was encircled by police fearing 'militants'. We emerged in small groups to find flashing lights and weapons drawn; but blood did not spill. For all our cries of 'By any means necessary' we of Harvard's Association of African and Afro-American Students had not been all that partial to blood, had voted down following the example of our brothers at Cornell University by smuggling of guns onto campus. We decided against storming that construction site, understanding it to be a suicide mission without adequate defensive weapons, because we'd believed in our futures. We had futures to believe in; and here I was now in Palestine, observing and speaking with people for whom 'life and death' has been bloody and real, whose presents and future were caged, yet were refusing to taint music's joy with the residues of conflict while we cultural nationalists spoke and some of us still speak of Their music and Our music. *A philosophy I fear that has ossified into entitlement. As counter-productive, even pernicious as the Israeli settlements I now so decry? Proud, seemingly impregnable, but ultimately arrogant, counter-productively aggressive and just, simply, wrong?*

A confident cascade of classical piano played with idiosyncratic enthusiasm suffuses the air as Iyad and I finish our conversation. This is sixteen year-old Mohammed, after five years of study one of Al Kamandjâti's major success stories. During my afternoon in Jenin I hear him switch comfortably from classical to jazz-style piano, play the accordion in an Oriental ensemble and am told that he's trying his hand at the mandolin. The normal attention per child is one or two private lessons per week plus two group sessions of solfeggio instruction and orchestra but Mohammed, who hopes to follow Ramzi's footsteps to the conservatory in Angers, spends every spare hour at the Jenin center. The teachers are happy to feed his enthusiasm and thus his sense of personal freedom, and thereby by osmosis perhaps, as the Mohammeds develop and mul-

tiply, the teachers' own, the town's, the nation's sense of freedom. Music's power dissolving borders, suffusing souls.

On the road from Nablus back to Ramallah that evening a snapshot of
parallels and paradoxes in the spirit of the book of that name comprised of
conversations between Daniel Barenboim and Edward Said:

Weary but content after a long afternoon of lessons and a stop for a
renowned area sweet, each of us in our own private reverie until the van comes
to a stop. Up ahead an Israeli military jeep and a small private car. The
inhabitants of both are young men and all are standing in a loose circle star-
ing at the ground. Our driver, a Palestinian father of three who looks to be
in his late thirties, goes out to investigate and returns to report that a wild
boar has been hit by the passenger vehicle, is mortally injured but not yet dead,
a situation he finds mildly amusing. The boar is hidden from our view by the
Israeli soldiers and the Palestinian youths, all of whom are smoking and
prodding the beast with their feet as they discuss what to do. One can feel no
urgency. I imagine the boar's heaving sides and quivering nostrils, eyes glazed,
near blind with pain, and the glistening, viscous blood upon which it must lie.
I feel that it should be put out of its misery. I can understand that under the
circumstances of history and geography, shooting it is not the best option.
Should someone drive over its skull? Grisly, yes, but faster than dragging it
out of the road and shoving it into the ravine, and how extraordinary that
these two groups of usual enemies, Israeli conscripts and Palestinian young
men out on the road just trying to live have found commonality, however
briefly, over the fate of a beast whose flesh is religiously forbidden to both.

Those of us in the van hear a shared chuckle from around the boar and
my two young female companions, a teacher of violin and viola from England
and a flautist from Tuscany are beside themselves. Touched to their core by
the animal's plight, mortified by the casual attitude of all at the scene, they
beseech our driver to do something and berate him for the callousness of his
attitude. There is nothing he can do. After a period that is undoubtedly far
shorter than it seems, he and the Greek teacher of oud and percussion climb
back into the van and we head towards Ramallah. For the remainder of our
drive the delicate young Italian girl is sobbing and the bright and straight-for-

ward English girl, who has defied a conservative, anti-Arab father to teach at Al Kamandjâti, is lecturing the driver about his lack of compassion to which the driver doesn't respond. His shoulders are steady as he transports his passengers who have so many more choices than does he or his family. I say nothing because I've just met these young people, admire their obvious commitment and have no wish to dampen their passions, but I can't help but consider that perhaps their concern for the boar is an indication of the relative lack of conflict in their backgrounds. The odds are overwhelming that all of the young men at the scene and our driver have lost people in this region's constantly roiling state of war. Our driver most certainly has experienced bombardment, anger and deprivation. All have stared violent human death in the face and dealt with its consequences so in comparison the misfortune of a boar is hardly cause for a crisis of their souls. When these young women have been longer in the world perhaps they'll have more tolerance of its greys. I will not shame them now. In retrospect I wonder if their distress for the boar wasn't a displacement of their stress at inhabiting so fraught a world, a place where nothing is without rippling repercussion.

As the days progress I become friendly with Julia, Al Kamandjâti's primary vocal instructor, a former student of archaeology in her early thirties so on the older side of Kamandjâti's European cadre. She is as tall as I am with long flowing red gold hair which she generally covers with a turquoise shawl for she is wholeheartedly embracing Palestinian life and its language and in her own original manner investigating Islam. We are an out of the ordinary pair striding the narrow stone sidewalks of Ramallah's hilly streets but again we arouse no inordinate interest, far, far less than was ever my lot in Central Europe's bastions of classical music, even after dark when the young men of Ramallah tend to travel in cheerful packs. In truth I've never felt so safe in the streets and later I am told that the West Bank crime rate is indeed very low, a partial reason for which being that there are few visible indicators between the have and the have-nots, consumer choice yet another victim of the occupation. Decent clothes and shoes are available in abundance in small shops and market stalls but there's very little variation in quality and style. Until I visited the Al-Amari refugee camp I saw no difference in the clothing worn by Al Kamandjâti's children of professionals and the children of laborers (and in fact marveled at all their abilities to unearth distinctive pocketing and embroidery in the piles of jeans that looked nondescript to my eyes). Unlike what I've been shown of other Arab countries, Ramallah's more well-off women do not bling with expensive jewellery and footwear. So instead of what I've been told of Cairo and know of London and São Paolo, where divisions between haves and have-nots percolate with undercurrents of envy and even rage, more the equanimity I've sensed in Copenhagen and Amsterdam.

Julia introduces me to a special friend, Saed (not his real name) a long-time member of the PLO's inner circle and recently retired minister of the Palestinian authority. The son of a farmer, Saed earned a university degree in literature and during his decades of exile in Cairo, Budapest and Beirut he compiled and lost libraries that contained thousands of books. He had a music library as well, more transportable in its cassette tape format, much of which was Western classical music seemingly recorded from various radio broadcasts. Our dinner was in the brand new apartment he would be sharing with his student daughter. Though a vast number of boxes had yet to be unpacked much of his music was readily accessible and we devoured our couscous to the weak strains of a Beethoven piano concerto. With our after-dinner arak, we were offered a gypsy ensemble, self-recorded by Saed during exile in Budapest where he and a few other PLO colleagues found communion with the small band that spent its evenings regaling moneyed Soviet apparatchiks. After hours the band, Saed and his comrades would soothe the aches of displacement with shared music, a smoke and a glass. The qualities of the play, like that of the Beethoven, were difficult to discern on the now stretched and eviscerated tapes, but its meaning to Saed shared as generously as the ample fare. *'You are welcome.'*

A quick-witted man with the darkest of humors, upon the establishment of the Palestinian Authority's ministry of education Saed had tried to donate his music library to the new state, but the minister in question had no interest, as ever the recovery of land and sovereignty being the priority rather than the life of the soul. Saed had heard of Al Kamandjâti but hadn't visited until two days after the dinner when picking up Julia and myself for a brief drive through his countryside. He was interested but betrayed no emotion as he was introduced to Ramzi, surveyed the courtyard with its eager young students, heard the strains of tentative practice drifting about from various rooms; and I could not help but be reminded of Martin Luther King, Jr.'s last speech in Memphis, Tennessee. *'I may not get there with you. But I want you to know tonight that we as a people will get to the Promised Land...'* The resonances between the African-American and Palestinian experiences were becoming ever more strong, yet here again, I find this veteran of hot and cold wars unencumbered by cultural polemic in his appreciation of the musics that have brought him both solace and exhilaration.

In Ramallah another success story, Mahmoud on violin, firing off an accomplished first portion of Vivaldi's Four Seasons without score just stretching his fingers with adolescent swagger and a glorious grin, also having studied for five years and also making good initial steps toward the playing of jazz. There are others who were referred to but whom I didn't hear, such as a girl pianist in Jenin torn between devoting her life to music or medicine. A number of adolescent young men excelling at various forms of Oriental percussion under the quietly demanding Ibrahim, drawn to that mode of expression like so many disenfranchised young men of diverse ethnicities are drawn to channeling their aggressions into potency by way of stretched skins over hollowed vessels, wooden sticks onto solid forms. The weekly meeting of the ninety-strong Al Kamandjâti orchestra combined players of mixed abilities making their way through Grieg's 'Hall of the Mountain King' with equivalent amounts of chaos and joy, which is not to say that there are no cultural challenges.

Particularly in the refugee camps entrée to choral singing and the beginnings of trust is achieved by working with Arab music before venturing into Western scores, but it would seem that more formidable is instilling a feeling for music in those for whom it has at most been tangential to their lives. When heard, on cheap televisions and radios, on poor bootleg cds, broadcast with distortion into environments awash with the clangs of desperate survival, music is never near its most compelling. Many of Al Kamandjâti's children have neither been sung to nor sung themselves before entering its programs. While the odd disco has begun to crop up for the life-grabbing youth of Ramallah and other less conservative outposts of Palestine, dancing has never been an intrinsic part of Palestinian culture save for the traditional *dabke*, a line dance performed at times of celebration usually only by men and not so often after 1948. So two of the most basic requirements for the making of music, a familiarity with pitch and rhythm and thus pacing, phrasing must be learned as a new and sometimes arcane language is learned. Combined with a lack of home practicing particularly in the refugee camps progress can be very slow and I have nothing but the utmost admiration for Al Kamandjâti's instructors, particular the young Westerners among whom there is absolutely no sense of cultural imperialism, rather a generosity of time and heart, living an adventure but not an easy one. It is early days for Al Kamandjâti, and it has teething problems that can't be unexpected for something without precedent in an environment fraught with perils of all kinds; but with its mission of replacing the daily violence suffered by the children of Palestine with culture and joy, there can be no argument. While I on my flight to Tel Aviv had used music to hunker down into myself, as a surrounding barrier wall, for the children of Al Kamandjâti music is their alternative to, their defiance of walls. It is their attachment of wings.

My return to London on a quiet Sunday evening is far less fraught than my departure. In my terminal of Ben Gurion Airport most surprising muzak filling its spacious modernity, selections from Mozart's Requiem masterfully exemplifying the soul's ascent from darkness into light. In this land of relentless turmoil, music. Unfinished and sublime.

'I wrote 20 lines about love
and imagined
this siege
has withdrawn 20 meters'
Mahmoud Darwish

Upon hearing me tell of my Ramallan idyll a sage half-smile from young Karim Said. 'But of course you know it can change in a minute,' and of course it did and it does. Not long after my second meeting with Karim came the report of the Israeli government's refusal to pay the medical expenses of a Jewish-American student who suffered a fractured jaw and the loss of an eye when hit by a tear gas canister during demonstrations at the Qalandia checkpoint, this in response to the Israeli storming of the flotilla attempting to breech the siege of Gaza which had resulted in the deaths of nine peace activists on board. Witnesses testify that the canister was fired directly into the young woman's face, this probably taking place while teachers of Al Kamandjâti were conducting music workshops in the Qalandia refugee camp directly adjacent to the checkpoint and the wall as they have been through countless previous manifestations of this struggle and will be for the countless more that will come.

9

Darkness into Light

March 2010. Not long after my return to London from Ramallah and Al Kamandjâti, I learn of a German-produced documentary film entitled Kinshasa Symphony just beginning to make the festival rounds. Having spent some days in that city five years before, I cannot imagine how this can be. I am not intrepid. The stubbornly elusive second novel had as a central element the conflict diamond trade in central Africa. There are numerous evocative accounts of the Congo/Zaire, Heart of Darkness of course, Naipul's Bend in the River and more empathetically Barbara Kingsolver's Poisonwood Bible, as well as reportage galore but I'd needed to smell the air, feel the humidity, see the river for myself however briefly. After months of seeking a protective umbrella for the trip an opportunity arose that necessitated my arrival within a week. I lied to obtain a visa. Rumor had it that the Democratic Republic of Congo wasn't partial to 'writers' so I was a broken-hearted woman seeking to heal herself by visiting all the major rivers of the world. A friend of the family had been living in Kinshasa but was about to be transferred and the Congo River was an absolute necessity in my quest. I don't know if the consular official believed me anymore than my father had believed my adolescent excuses for curfew violations way back when but, three days later I was on my way.

Passenger flights from Europe tend to arrive just before Kinshasa's lightening quick equatorial dusk. Shadows were long as we disembarked from the plane and near extinguished by the time we entered the airline hanger serving as immigration. As I was to find everywhere in that city, there was no system. Hustlers offered their services to help you through the confusion of entry, for a price. There were no lines to speak of so one took on the obligation to progress and recede such as one could via a combination of deference and chutzpah. My ability to speak French ebbed and flowed as necessary. It helped that I'd read a few guides and was tall with elbows that easily moved in proximity to Adam's apples. On the other side of the murk the parking lot was filled with vendors hawking bananas and hard-boiled eggs, porters in faded pink coveralls and young men with AK 47s guarding citizens as they went to their cars.

It was rush hour as we headed into the city and total anarchy to my eyes: very few streetlights, the odd naked bulb shining above the set of white plastic chairs before some kind of emporium, no traffic lights and, again, no system. The road was characterized by huge potholes and ruts. Vehicles got stuck — many of them minivans stuffed to the point of cartoon absurdity with Kinois who have no other transport from point A to point B, often with no windows and a rear door held open by one strong arm to allow some ventilation. There were no buses. Others tried to move forward however they could, and nobody took it upon themselves to loosen any resultant impasse, but also no exasperated vituperations, very few soundings of horns; instead an eerily quiet stoicism. Characteristic of the Kinois as I would learn, who have virtually nothing and no one on their side save for themselves and their God, and indispensable for any approximation of sanity.

That an orchestra, the Orchèstre Symphonique Kimbanguiste, should be playing Western classical music, in this place with no infrastructure to speak of and so at the mercy of a climate most inhospitable to the majority of symphonic instruments, with no economy to speak of, the most rudimentary of educations available, how, how were they managing this? And with such a rich tradition and present of dynamic popular music, music that evolved from the region's pre-colonial rain forest and savannah with the help of Cuban influence into *soukous* and *kwassa-kwassa,* music that I heard coming from all directions in the *cités* when I was there and has often provided an organized alternative living space — at once emotive and reflective — for those who have no choice but to inhabit a world devoid of dependable contours, why were they identifying with, even needing this Western classical music?

What I see in the film is little changed from my short time four years before its filming: vehicles belching exhaust as they traverse near impassable roads that have received no maintenance since the Belgians left in 1961. Rubble, refuse, constant cacophony and citizens making their way resolutely through the daily challenge of sustaining life, somehow managing neat appearance and dignity amidst a vortex of chaos; but also what I found hard to envision: an assemblage of near one hundred players rehearsing Beethoven's Ninth Symphony within a makeshift green plastic enclosure with no roof, dripping perspiration in the tropical night heat, squinting at their scores when the generator-provided electric power dimmed the small naked light bulbs, plagued by a variety of insects after day jobs as seamstresses, hairdressers, barbers, cooks often with inadequate food in their bellies. I watch string players: a cellist, a violist catching practice time during respective work breaks outside against a background of traffic noise and exhaust. I see a chorus member slowly translating Schiller's German in the 'Ode to Joy' into French for the group understanding, struggling with the German sounds, commenting on the difficulty in the local dialect of Lingala, and not giving up. The orchestra manager building string instruments from raw wood purchased in a local market and patterns derived from taking previously obtained instruments apart; young orchestra members coaxing doubtful friends to give their music a try by coming to their concert. Passages of Beethoven are near shambolic as the predominantly self-taught players stumble their way forward, talking about how the music transports them to a place all their own, free from care. They are near defeat two evenings before performance but pull it out somehow to an enthusiastic audience of two thousand in an open space surrounded by dance halls that have agreed to mute their own music for the duration. Ecstatically moving, soul-enhancing stuff and even more so given what the film hadn't time to explore.

It is mentioned that the self-taught conductor, former airline pilot Armand Diangienda is the grandson of Simon Kimbangu, founder of the Kimbanguist church, a Protestant denomination now followed by 10 per cent of the population of the Democratic Republic of Congo, but the filmmakers don't explore the fact the Orchestre Symphonique Kimbanguiste (OSK) established in 1994 is predominantly a manifestation of worship by church members. In the words of Diangienda 'the orchestra didn't come together to earn a wage but to glorify God', its members not seeing it therefore as a possible means to better earthly opportunities. Many Congolese churches have orchestras but save for the exception of the OSK all are salvation-tinged variations on popular musical styles, with instrumental accompaniment an assortment of brass and predominantly electric guitar. Subtly intricate guitar is a characteristic of Congolese popular music, players often fashioning their own beginning acoustical instruments out of a variety of receptacles and any wire at hand; but in an environment so hostile to their survival, there were few Western orchestral string instruments to be found when the OSK began, five violins shared among twelve players learning what they could in twenty minute intervals. Diangienda's grandfather founded the Church of Christ on Earth by His Special Envoy Simon Kimbangu in 1921. Faith healing was his immediate calling card, but his message of 'Black will become white and white will become black' so threatened the ruling Belgians that he was imprisoned but five months after his ministry began, a death penalty commuted to a life sentence that lasted thirty years.

The religion cum-movement was kept alive during that period first by Kimbangu's wife and then by their son, Diangienda's father Joseph. Its principle tenets, alongside love, the Bible, work and 'inspired singings' were anti-colonialism, African nationalism and, once this was realized, the reconstitution of the *bakongo-lari* black identity, African identity. To this must be added the fact that all members of the orchestra beyond their teens would have experienced the Authenticité policies of fallen dictator Mobutu Sese Seko: 'discovering [their] personality by reaching into the depths of [their] past for rich cultural heritage left to [them] by [their] ancestors', which encompassed first names, by law changed from Christian to African. In dress the wise choice for men was the *abacost,* collarless two piece ensembles with cravat (from the French *à bas le costume!)* and, for women, modest pagnes and tops rather than Western dress. In the arts, again as with Stasov's Russia and my own Black Arts Movement, there were stylistic encouragements as to what embodied Zaïrois. Interesting then that Armand Diangienda first became captivated by Western classical music by the constant playing of Handel's Messiah in his father's private home.

There are those in the DRC who feel that the established Kimbanguist Church, which was legalized by the Belgians in 1957 then embraced by Mobutu during his regime, is straying too far from its remit towards African cultural identity.

Apostolic splinter churches are forever sprouting up in Kinshasa proclaiming closer adherence to the spirit of the Founder, but his grandson the conductor, who is addressed as Papa and bowed down to by the faithful, has extended his spiritual home via music from the realm of the colonial oppressor, finding through it a means to further extend African identity. Of late he has been turning his hand to composition and arrangement, seeking to meld the Western classical and African musical traditions into one. Armand Diangienda has his own personal artistic aspirations, but it would seem that for the majority of his musicians, the majority of his flock, the music of Beethoven, Mozart, Verdi and Orff rather than that of Tabu Ley Rochereau has simply blessed their souls with flight in a locale so many associate with the heart of turgid, devouring darkness. Like Ramzi and Iyad in Palestine they see no paradox in their embrace of an art form birthed in the land of colonial oppressors. They have no time or space for idle discourse. They need and so they do, with all that they have.

Kinshasa Symphony the film is directed towards Western audiences and cannot help but appeal with its portrait of a materially impoverished people doing for themselves without recourse to Western aid but using as currency the results of individual Western genius. I tend to discern a 'dancing-bear' sentimentality in such situations: it's not that the bear dances well but that he dances at all. Isn't it heart-warming — and reassuring — to see how hard these colored folks are trying even as they fail?

The OSK really can't play as advantaged Western orchestras can play and the tone of their catch-as-catch-can instruments is harsh. The evening after my first viewing of the film I attended a concert by the London Symphony Orchestra and was thrust backwards by the comparative richness of the sound: the standard of the play, the rich excellence of the instruments, the complexity of interpretation. No comparison really; but my cynicism in regards to the content of this film is stilled by the sheer strength of the depicted communion between human spirits, that of the Congolese Orchestre and Beethoven, the Orchestre and Verdi and Ravel. Across time, distance and consistently destructive history, members of the Orchestre Symphonique Kimbanguiste is discovering beauty and holding it fast with neither time nor energy wasted deconstructing the worthiness of its source. Who was I in my privileged comfort to question the source of so transcendental a joy?

10

Opera in the Streets

Continuing my idiosyncratic perambulation, I attend a singing workshop in an East London services center for the homeless run by Streetwise Opera.

Streetwise was initiated by former 'not very good' music student and later music journalist Matt Peacock, who was volunteering at a shelter in 2002 when an MP described the homeless as the people you stepped over when you came out of the opera house. The outraged Peacock decided to upend some tables. The outcome in the years since: from its first activities at a night shelter in Westminster, Streetwise has expanded to encompass weekly sessions at eleven homeless centers in several English cities, among the results of which have been prize-winning live productions and films combining the talents of homeless participants with dedicated and innovative professionals. Described by a journalist as resembling 'a raggedy Tintin' in his drive to provide for needs of the homeless beyond the obvious practicalities of roof and board, the youthful Peacock has been showered with garlands and accolades which have done nothing to mitigate his fervour. I become intrigued by the program after hearing him speak at one of the plethora of conferences on cultural policy wont to crop up about London.

The sun is encouragingly bright through industrial or institutional-sized windows. The folk I watch gather are a disparate lot, male and female, primarily Caucasian but from a number of countries (I'm told that the homeless of color tend more toward the West End shelters). It is difficult to judge the ages of those whose bodies have been so unprotected, but I approximate from early twenties to maybe forties though Streetwise encompasses many who are older. Some are confident and eager, some more tentative; all are clean. A table offers simple snacks, biscuits, grapes. We begin. Simple observation is not allowed so I join the circle for the opening vocalization exercises which to my ear moves from chanting plainsong to something akin to the minimalism of John Adams as we use the syllables of our names and the phrase 'I saw a dog' to ease open our thoraxes. There are two professionals present (leaders? teachers?) one at an electric keyboard, the other a circulating cheerleader. Would that my voice were so flexible as my ear! I'm not very good and having shown willing am allowed to bow out and take note as the session moves to introductory work on a coming performance of Stephen Sondheim's Into the Woods. As well as voices, bodies stiffened by nights on inhospitable surfaces loosen as the workshop members weave in and out of patterns as they sing. At the break an ex-copywriter fallen on bad times explains to me that while he loves Haydn he still hasn't developed an ear for Benjamin Britten and how the singing coincides with the beats of his heart.

The definition of the word opera is straight-forward enough: a dramatic work of one or more acts set to music for singers and instrumentalists, from the Italian for labor, but the social and cultural baggage that has accompanied the art form from its courtly beginnings straight up through the twentieth century, save for the odd examples of a Beggars' Opera, a Magic Flute, Carmen and the brief pause during the early stages Italian *verismo* opera presentation, has been heavy and elitist in the extreme. In the frustrating early stages of Gareth Malone Goes to Glyndebourne in which the irrepressible chorus master selects and prepares a primarily working class teenage chorus to sing in the premiere of a contemporary opera in the verdant hills of East Sussex, Malone remarks that 'sometimes I think it would be better if we just didn't use the word opera.' Similarly in speaking of one of his projects for children composer Jonathan Dove wrote 'We didn't actually call it an opera because we didn't want to put people off' though the piece in question was through-composed with both opera singers and singing actors. At mere mention of the word a great many people of all descriptions are ready to scramble towards braids of garlic and silver stakes, but without the trappings of bourgeois one-upmanship, with impassioned execution intent on human connection, often ecstatic human connection, artificial boundaries are innumerably traversed and why not? For are we not a species programmed for music and narrative, with language one of our crowning achievements? With this in mind, how many things more attractively visceral and glorious than an amalgam of all three?

The contemporary impulse towards defusing opera's forbidding airs is hardly the first. During the Weimar period in Germany *Zeitoper,* particularly in its Hindemith, Krenek and Brecht/Weill manifestations, was devoted to amending the genre's bourgeois connotations, rendering it more democratic and accessible to the common man, but in the main, Dreigröschenoper aside, their efforts seldom penetrated beyond the artistic elites. More than distancing themselves from the discredited and sentimental excesses of the Wilhelmine era, they also refused to own or purvey any on-stage passions of their own. Works such as Jonny spielt auf and Neues vom Tage offered oh-so-sophisticated cynicism and disdain when what was craved by their hard-pressed audiences was strong universal emotions with which they could identify or barring these, escapism, pure, simple or extravagant in a multitude of varieties. This akin to the compensatory craving for throw pillows, carved wood and sentimental ornament when confronted with the spare and hard-edged architectural recommendations of such as Corbusier's 'machine for living' public housing and the more rigorous public proposals from the Bauhaus School of the same period. I am familiar with this impulse, for Bauhaus principles were the guiding covenant behind Harvard's undergraduate design courses during my time there.

Many of the professors in the then newly configured Department of Visual and Environmental Studies, my chosen major, were Central European refugees from the Bauhaus invited to Cambridge by Walter Gropius, former head of the Graduate School of Architecture now bearing his name. They were very happy to be there and equally happy to continue their Weimar approach to the cosmos. A good deal of our studio work involved esoterically described design problems that generally took me days to approximate let alone answer. My favorite design instructor was a Japanese whose command of English was limited and therefore taught by quietly centered example. Zen vs. Bauhaus if you will. The department was housed in Corbusier's only North American building which we were compelled to study in detail. I found its celebrated surfaces bereft of human consideration (and was reminded of all of this during a recent touring retrospective exhibition of the master's oeuvre) but in my politics was happy to share the similarly elitist Black Nationalist dictates towards our own *Lumpenproletariet*, who in our interpretation were too beaten down by The System to know what was best for them. During the *Zeitoper* heyday, as often now, the artistic leanings of the common man were often the object of similar condescension by creative elites — '*They don't know what's good for them.*' '*They don't know what art is.*' — when emotional honesty without trappings, be they rococo swags or self-indulgently ugly rigor, will reach and penetrate all.

My first live encounter with Cecilia Bartoli. I have the privilege of sitting

*second row center. She will be singing Haydn concert arias. I've heard her
recordings before, mostly on radio while driving the motorways of Southern
California, but I am not prepared. My heart races, my eyes are moist, my arms
tingling, and through my quivering synapses the certainty that any South
Central Los Angeles gang member, Latino, Crip or Blood confronted with her
power would feel exactly the same as I do now. Were they so lucky as I they
would be on their feet, all notions of cool abandoned, whooping and hollering
for this European coloratura with her feet planted firmly on the stage, her voice
and arms pulling them, us into her embrace with no need for translation of any
kind. She is human. They are human. We are human. It is simple.*

Like most prominent companies New York's Metropolitan
Opera has a thriving education department and has discovered
that for the City's primarily black and Latino public secondary
school students the Italian operas especially have a major
appeal, which is not so difficult to understand. To young lives
characterized by unharnessed passions and violence the Italian
plots aren't absurd excess but day-to-day reality, the incandescent high notes an accurate mirror of their own emotions, the
floor-vibrating basses an embodiment of doom without
redemption with which they are all too familiar. Given the
opportunity to create their own operas, how far removed the
traditions of recitative from the narrative modes of hip-hop
and rap? How difficult to find and expand their lives with
opera?

For the six hundred who regularly attend Streetwise sessions, who are young and old, Brits of all description, Eastern
Europeans, Africans, a full reflection of England's multi-cultural stew, life has been re-discovered, access and structure now
given to time and environments previously bereft of under-
standable signposts and human contact. If they don't want to
solo they can sing in groups; if they don't want to sing in public
at all they can work on costumes and scenery. Increased self-
esteem, the positive and sustained human interactions conse-

quent with being a Streetwise participant often aids in their becoming more trusting, more organized, enough to acquire such basics as a safe and clean living space of their own, sometimes employment; and while the participants are exposed to all kinds of vocal music, not just opera, Peacock attests that 'the overwhelming majority love opera the most.'

I send away for the first Streetwise cd. There's a Place for Us, Somewhere. That song from West Side Story is featured along with selections by Mozart, Shostakovich, Bizet, Gershwin and Dvorak some with lyrics modified to purpose, generally translated into English, sometimes reworked to annotate the particularities of homeless experience. Workshop leaders sometimes lend their professional voices to those of their students but it is the homeless who arrest. With compromised dentistry and muscles only just acquainted with the demands of lyric projection, enunciation is often problematic. One can hear that lungs have been ravaged by elements environmental and self-administered. There is a commonality in the rasp of their voices with country blues singers and farmer-preachers of the American South, with the rail-riding guitar-picking hobos recorded by musical anthropologist Alan Lomax in the 1930s, in the staggeringly eloquent late recordings of Billie Holiday, all of them serrated by lives experienced with limited mercy using notes and words assembled by others to convey truths they've only just now been learning how to tell.

At the reception following a presentation of the current work in progress a young man from Nottingham who'd slept rough for two years describes opera as giving him life. He has just been singing and he is aglow. In Streetwise Opera the music associated with courtly diversion, with bourgeois self-congratulation, is transfigured into an art for survival and thereby honored.

11

A Brief Pause to Take Stock

(I sit on a bench and consider)

Al Kamandjâti, Streetwise Opera, the Orchestre Kimbanguiste are but three examples of music, some of which could and has been characterized as that of the racial, colonial and/or class oppressor, enhancing even transporting lives lived in extremis with no energy wasted in debate as to the origins of that joy. The birthplace of its composers is not considered grounds for its dismissal. Time isn't allocated to determine whether or not its embrace is a Trojan horse of insidious neo-imperialisms bound to eliminate what is pure, noble and, above all, native to its celebrants. Its power and wonder is enough. For all my professed objectivity and vows that I would not allow the prism of my history distort my view, I am a twentieth-century artefact/veteran of culture wars, and this is not what I expected.

I'd expected said wars to be more pervasive in their grip, oblivious to geography, oblivious to time, mutating to accommodate environmental differences but tenacious. I was pleased to be wrong, while noting to myself, that these three and others similar are valiant efforts but small. We who care about matters cultural, educational and political, admire if we notice, maybe help if we can, seldom imagining that there could be something here for us to learn; for we in the privileged multicultural West are by and large complacent in our privilege. Particularly in the United States and the United Kingdom, we have burdened ourselves with a tremendous excess of cultural baggage. We are obese with our territorialities, our cultural gang wars with their stylized masques of respect and countervailing struggles for precedence and financial endowment. We parse and label. Who has suffered the most and therefore earned more munificent compensation? Who is the Best?

It was my sense before embarking on the current venture that these skirmishes are as detrimental to our cultural health as our overly sumptuous and too often nutritionally empty gastronomies are to our physical selves, and I've become more impassioned. I'm perceiving arteries clogging with prejudices, affronts and hegemonic impulses. There was a time when acknowledgment and support of diversities was necessary for our health. In its purity it still is and always will be, *I hear Aretha singing. 'Respect!'* but as is happening with our physical beings, so much of what was once revolutionary nourishment has become intransigent and stodgy. In this new century, to resist the urgencies of shape-shifting dynamics, to resist new food stuffs for new global realities, rendering the suppleness of our cultural lives, is to put our very souls at risk. We lumber and bellow on any number of barricades, but impeded by our glut, are too often loath to explore the new or barely known — which might involve a divestment of credo and any number of other familiarities — and thereby miss much.

Pattern and complacency can be so comfortable, and we are abetted in our lack of curiosity by the cultural industries of the US and the like-minded UK in particular with their emphasis on monetary success and skill at every turn. In encouraging even enforcing a rigidity of stylistic categories, often based upon ethnicity and race, to better focus their marketing efforts. An overweening homogenized pop style epitomized by gladiatorial X-Factors and various Idols is their triumph, shows far more about acquisition, vicarious dreams and aggressions than about music. Said shows have been described by punk and pop historian Jon Savage as being for 'people who aren't passionate about music', with the aside that 'there's always been a huge market for people who aren't passionate about music.' Not that there haven't been talent shows for the better part of a century if not longer that have launched the careers of wonderful artists, Ella Fitzgerald for one Gladys Knight for another. It's the glitzy commercialism geometrically enhanced by technological prestidigitations here that forges alarm in those who dissent from its template of success as it fosters an unquestioning herd mentality in both audience and participant, where ultimately all is about money and Fame with music *of the heart of the spheres of the soul* barely discernible if not totally obscured.

We are distracted, we privileged folk; narcissistic as well. Taking our own context as the entire world's default position we perpetuate a cultural arrogance many of us fought to pulverize, *our memories are so short*, thinking that with our seemingly limitless abilities to know and to analyze all innovation, *ignorant as well as arrogant*, all recipes for a meaningful contemporary life will be of our own devising, and surely not from countries or environments we consider impoverished, conflicted and backwater. We are therefore astonished by what has occurred in Venezuela.

12

Manna from the South

A youth orchestra of unfamiliar hues, the hair glistening and dark rather than blonde and sandy, the complexions burnished ivory and amber to teak rather than chalk, peach or strawberries and cream. *Much of my life regulated by skin color first and foremost, I am acutely, viscerally aware.* The demeanor alert, but also relaxed in their pre-performance postures, anticipatory smiles rather than the sense of nerves being overcome. First a Shostakovich 10 that staggered with its precision and intensity. So confident a command of Stalin's dour nemesis was unexpected from tawny youths of the Southern Hemisphere. Audience postures become alert. This band has come to play and play they do in all senses of the word. After the interval Latin rhythms, by way of the Jewish Broadway and Harvard cross-pollinating genius of Leonard Bernstein, Mexican composer José Pablo Moncayo and Argentinean Alberto Ginastera, and the dam of classical music deportment bursts its seams. The Orchestra under the baton of Gustavo Dudamel, their charismatic conductor since 1999 when he was a mere eighteen years old, has been moving into the music in a manner hitherto unknown by this seasoned and knowledgeable audience. In the encores they are performing Mexican waves with their instruments, playing pizzicati while dancing salsa, their basses are dipping and twirling dance partners, trumpets are spun like propellers, with technical precision and musicality never compromised for a nanosecond. And the audience is dancing, not just the Promenaders, those in the seats as well. Calvinist notions of the Devil's presence when the body moves in joyous rhythm banished for good and certain at least for this one night. At the concert's end the assembled are stomping and cheering in exultation, the youthful Latin faces radiant with joy and perhaps a slight wash of surprise for they have just been doing what they do, what many of them have been doing since the age or five and six, living in music and playing for their lives.

There are resonances, of the delirious European responses to Nijinsky's Rite of Spring, to Josephine Baker's bobbling brown breasts, to Fauvish color and early jazz, African masks and rock and roll. Release via the Primitive and often people of color from Northern cold and Protestant ethics, but always previously tamed or subsumed by changing fashions and the powers that have been. The Northern gestalt remaining triumphant for Progress is the god of the North (with all the accompanying dysfunction of Wotan and his clan) and Progress has always trumped Primitivism has it not? But these Venezuelans are not a simplistic triumph of the primitive. They are a new embodiment of a music reverenced in such halls, new life being breathed into the Canova perfection of an art form, exquisite but frequently more still than it might be and therefore accumulating webs, mists, other concealments. They are as messenger gods revealing a new way, youthful as such gods have generally been.

An increasingly open secret among music educators and a smattering of elite musicians since the late 1990s and gathering both strength and renown with its Jeunesse Musicale tours of Germany and Austria in 2000, 2002 and 2005 — *in the manner of a mid-Atlantic hurricane born of the tropical waters lapping Venezuela's northern coast travelling north across these warm waters, gathering and harnessing forces, making landfall to torrentially dramatic, irresistible effect* — Fundamusical and its ambassadorial flagship the Simón Bolívar Orchestra 'B' achieved tipping point in 2007 with the April announcement that Gustavo Dudamel would succeed Esa-Pekka Salonen as musical director of the Los Angeles Philharmonic, its UK appearances at the Proms and the Edinburgh Festival and an equally incandescent autumn tour of the United States.

As is often the way in the thrall of such excitement, the decades of dedicated and charismatic leadership by its founder José Antonio Abreu; personal commitment on the part of both teachers and children; as well as the financial and political commitment of the Venezuelan government were not the focus as arts ministers and classical aficionados clamored for similar efforts to be introduced 'here and now'. The facts that Fundamusical has been considered in Venezuela as first and foremost a force for social cohesion, betterment — indeed, often literal salvation; that it is financed via the President's office — rather than sloughed off to a secondary ministry; were often swept to the side by feverish hopes that in Fundamusical's El Sistema a means of re-establishing classical music as an integral component of contemporary Western culture. At long last a magic elixir had been uncovered that would refigure Western classical music away from the backwater for the antique, the rich and the idiosyncratic that it was increasingly becoming. Awards were showered, documentaries were filmed, conferences and seminars were held, programs planned and initiated. With Dudamel set to take up his appointment in autumn 2009, the Los Angeles Philharmonic led the way in autumn 2007 with the establishment of the Youth Orchestra of Los Angeles (YOLA) as an ES-modeled addendum to a long-established but fairly elite constellation of regional youth orchestras. The Baltimore Symphony Orchestra followed closely behind with its Orchkids initiative in 2008.

As a recipient of the TED Prize in 2009, José Antonio Abreu's 'One Wish to Change the World' resulted in the creation of the Abreu Fellows Program at the New England Conservatory of Music. The first class of ten postgraduate musicians dedicated to the propagation of El Sistema seedlings into the Northern Hemisphere completed their study and internship in Venezuela in the spring of 2010 and are currently establishing ES centers or nucleos in Boston, Philadelphia, Atlanta, Georgia; Corona, Queens, New York; Durham, North Carolina and Juneau, Alaska with other cities in earlier stages of becoming. After two years of investigation and planning El Sistema Scotland initiated its first Big Noise program in the deprived Raploch area of Stirling in the summer of 2008 with a view toward opening three more centers by 2013. In autumn 2009 England's El Sistema-inspired In Harmony opened three centers targeting similar communities in Lambeth, Liverpool and Norwich. As is characteristic of their arts funding systems, the majority of the U.S. nucleos have been launched with private sponsorship, with minimal or no public supplement, while those in the UK have received time-limited (at this writing three year) government grants but in the current economic reality are actively seeking other streams of support.

'There is something magically powerful and transformative about classical music. We're not arguing that it's the only thing and that everyone should drop what they're doing, but we're not going to apologize for engaging kids with the very best music that humans have created...'

Mark Slavkin, Vice President of Education

Los Angeles Music Center New England Conservatory of Music,

El Sistema seminar, November 2007

Viewed on an internet-posted video of the NEC conference during the earliest stages of my research on El Sistema, Mr. Slavkin's comment was as toreador's cape to my Pavlovian bull and prime catalyst for my ensuing quest. I rankled and heaved, boring myself with my predictability. 'Is this the attitude guiding those formulating El Sistema projects?' I asked myself, 'A perfunctory nod in the direction of cultural/political correctness utterly overwhelmed by dismissive and hierarchical thinking? Can they really in the twenty-first century, in their chosen professions, be so deluded as to believe that so patronizing an attitude will encourage the years of time-intensive commitment by children of color and the working class necessary to produce the results they desire and imagine? Is education their calling or indoctrination?

'And specifically in the United States, what about jazz? What happens to jazz education, the development and celebration of 'America's classical music,' music distilled from the blood and soul of my African-American people, if increasingly limited funds are faddishly diverted to Sistema clones?'

Twentieth century cultural combat redux, but *pace* Langston Hughes, I have been wondering as I wander, arthritically feeling my way onto a new terrain far more nuanced in its detail than the old black and white polarities well-flagged with blood red. In New York, the Director of Education at Jazz at Lincoln Center assuages my fears about jazz. Their concerns are building audiences and a love of jazz and working towards a viable jazz pedagogy, not how enthusiasms about El Sistema might affect their funding. They appreciate dedication to excellence in music wherever it can be found, and El Sistema personifies this pursuit of excellence. Before travelling to Venezuela I've spoken to the director of Baltimore's Orchkids and visited the programs in Raploch and Lambeth where it is far too early to know how the young participants will respond to cultural forces outside their Sistema refuges. Will its music remain 'their' music or will they be cajoled into folds more characteristic of their environments? Will they stay the course? Will their programs find the requisite funding to be there? But in no case did I find evidence of the Slavkin attitude. Rather dedicated zeal and in the continuous, encouraging attendance of bows scratching across open strings, far more patience than has ever been my gift. By the time of my arrival in Caracas I have removed my old chunks of triangular glass to a secured rear pocket of my brain, available should they be called for, but no longer my instruments of first perception. Where they belong.

Caracas is in thrall to the automobile. Oil is the prime mover of Venezuela's economy and petrol prices are astoundingly low. Most tanks can be completely refilled with change returned from the equivalent of a dollar and large, guzzling cars are de rigueur on a municipal highway system that was almost immediately rendered obsolete by an exponentially-increasing volume of traffic. Motorway progression is snail-paced at all times of the day, and no one seems to be interested in side streets or the time alternative routes might save. The abundance of smog reminds me of Los Angeles during the 1970s before air pollution regulations became stringent for both drivers and industry; the air sometimes became so bad that those with pulmonary disorders were told to remain inside and away from closed windows, that and the parched condition of the hills and parks. The area has been suffering from drought and there have been forest fires. Again like Los Angeles ashes from the flames have combined with low-lying marine layers from the adjacent sea to produce hours of grey gloom. I've eschewed my sun and sea winter break to make this journey and had been counting on a compensatory envelope of tropical heat. It isn't hot and the architecture is overwhelmingly late twentieth century Concrete Modern. Not beautiful then this city, but as suggested by Bolivar Orchestra members, its people more than compensate. Venezuela produces nearly as many winning beauty contestants as it does barrels of oil, the raw materials for which suffuse and delight the eye at every turn.

Though there are small pockets of unadulterated examples of Venezuela's three major racial components of indigenous, European and African, the vast majority of its population is *pardo*, that is an amalgam of all three. According to the popular description, 'everyone carries within them some part of the arrow and the drum.' There are some who've focused on Venezuela's essential if mongrel homogeneity as an important element in Fundamusical's success, that it hasn't been plagued with the often fraught protocols of multi-culti turf wars of any number of lands, but of course there are hierarchies here. Even were it not a basic truism of human settlement, with a history of conquest, slavery and liberation struggles that never fully wrested control of land and resources from colonial elites and lurking exterior vested interests all too common a story on this continent, how could there not be? While Venezuela no longer sports a European-origined oligarchy and its class/color lines are far more permeable than in many other Latin American cultures, the dominance of the light-complected in its positions of power has only recently begun to be broken. Caracas is now considered the murder capital of the world with eighty homicides of a weekend far from uncommon. So-called 'express kidnappings', quick, fairly inexpensive, terrifying, have been endemic since the turn of the millennium, relentless gang warfare a constant in the country's many barrios. What else are these unsettling statistics if not evidence of severe hierarchical unrest? However, there has always been music. Venezuelans are surrounded by music from the womb onwards and music has been a natural alternative vocabulary for many throughout its history. While so-called classical music has been a feature of particularly church culture since the early sixteenth century with home-grown composers generating their own works from very early on, as is ever the way the music of common people has been an accessible interplay of story-telling, sentiment and bravado in styles redolent of the nation's rich gumbo of bloodlines.

When José Antonio Abreu embarked on his evangelical mission in 1975 with the founding of Fundmusical's precursor Social Action for Music there were but two symphony orchestras in all of Venezuela, the vast majority of whose musicians were foreign born. Western classical music had not been a vibrant part of the national culture since the nineteenth century decades of civil conflict which reduced the country's population by one quarter to one third, a large percentage of which casualties were among what might be considered the cultural and economic elite, including classical musicians and their traditional patrons. While Abreu himself was a committed amateur musician harboring ambitious dreams for the prominence of Venezuela and indeed all of Latin America on classical music's global stage, his first priority was to offer the youth of his nation, particularly those for whom crime might be a first option, social, educational and spiritual alternatives to the chaos with which they were too often surrounded. A devout Catholic of conservative demeanor and unencumbered lifestyle, there is much of the innovative, enterprising (and formidable) abbot about Abreu and it is easy to imagine El Sistema as his own dynamic and cannily apolitical manifestation of the liberation theology that was sweeping through Latin America during Fundamusical's formative years. On its simplest level, Abreu's and thus El Sistema's philosophy is that the hand that holds a musical instrument cannot do the same with a gun or a knife, and more broadly, that the musical ensemble is concurrently both an individual and communal responsibility (and success if commitment is dedicated) and thus an ideal example of civic interaction. Also fundamental: that this ideal's desired incarnation is an excellence which is not easily obtained, can only be obtained through long and intensive application; yet can be obtained by all involved who give their all. This includes everyone, not only those who are preternaturally 'gifted', with resultant benefits to all of pride and joy. Such is the engine that has produced a miracle for our time. That this ideal is based on the ensemble/community, that Fundamusical is not in the business of developing individual virtuosi, is a revolutionary challenge to those cultures entranced by its product but more firmly entrenched in the pursuit of individual happiness and incandescence.

In Dr Richard Holloway, chair of El Sistema Scotland, former Bishop of Edinburgh and Scottish Arts Council chair, Raploch's Big Noise has a mature leader fully dedicated to the transfer of El Sistema's social mission to Scottish communities in dire need of its galvanizing power, one who speaks as well of the transformative miracle effected on Raploch's teachers as they convey their attention and expertise on hungering young charges. I wonder how El Sistema transplants will survive without such Master Gardeners. There is no denying that there is something of the religious about El Sistema. With or without obeisance to any other deity: the transfiguring power of the music, the dedication of all involved, the joy it affords participant and witness. Religion without the corruptions of power, but perhaps suspect to those for whom the 'I' is First King?

I have already been to the Simon Bolivar Conservatory of Music, the apex of Fundamusical's instructive system from which the majority of the travelling orchestras are drawn and to which dedicated students from remote parts of the country will travel for days by bus for special seminars. The Conservatory has no residential facilities. If need be students from the provinces sleep on floors. The intention is that the System will become less Caracas-centric, but for now it is their Rome or perhaps more aptly their Vienna or Chicago and so they come. Some of the rehearsal rooms have soundproofing, others do not. There is no quibbling, no resentments. Those in the System learn to work with and despite their environments. I encounter a jazz combo working through the dynamics of a seminal work by Charlie Parker, tracking its sound like a hound on a scent to discover two saxophone players, a guitarist and a drummer who are replicating the Parker recording note for note until they are joined by a female trumpet player, Linda Briceño who simply but voluptuously constructs her own sound.

Having written of a twentieth century jazz trumpeter and her travails I am entranced by Linda's casual certainty and dis-abused of my assumption that El Sistema is only about Western classical music. I am told that while Western classical music is the model because it offers a standardized method of progressing through levels and achievements of increasing complexity and presents persistent challenges, it is not held as the only music of value. Popular and folkloric music have always been used as a means to engage the very young and the characteristics of both have been profoundly affected by the ES graduates that have taken their classically-trained skills down non-classical routes: play of the ukulele-type *cuatro* has gone from mere strummed accompaniment to virtuosic in the manner that Jimi Hendrix and other electric guitar heroes transformed the instrumental hierarchy and very nature of rock and roll.

While Maestro Abreu's love and covenant has always been Western classical music, intrinsic to his brainchild is its obligation to be a living and progressive entity ever responsive to its participants' needs and desires. Folkloric music is highlighted in many of the Fundamusical's heartland nucleos. Abreu himself is now speaking of the formation of salsa orchestras where once he considered that music emblematic of his country's ills of chaos, crime and addiction, thus embodying the tenet of humility before his creation that in my experience of the System is a characteristic of all who are involved be they teachers or administrators, students or graduate 'stars'. Both Gustavo Dudamel and Edicson Ruiz, who at age seventeen became the youngest musician ever to join the Berlin Philharmonic, return regularly to Venezuela to teach and to play despite exterior suggestions that that part of their lives might be done with. To abandon what made them would be to tear themselves asunder. The Sistema is within them and cannot be expunged. *And so again the wash of religion.*

El Sistema's ecumenical attitude towards music, the fact that it is utilizing, developing, indeed honouring a plethora of styles is not the stuff of its headlines and reputation outside Latin America where journalists, those in the classical world and arts policy mavens clamor excitingly, even desperately about its redemptive potential for classical music alone. Too small print for them perhaps if indeed they are at all aware, but revelatory for me and already piquing the imaginations of the first ten Abreu Fellows who are completing their time in situ during my visit. Among them a clarinetist who dreams of developing a nucleo dedicated to the American Song Book, another to Texas with salsa, and still another wanting to push out the borders of hip-hop. *As apostles, spreading Good News.* Already I have learned that the hierarchically tinged comments of Mark Slavkin and others of common belief can be beside the point, for the System can be and already is many things to many people. *And moving me towards campground.*

My second day. I am driven by dry, grey-brown hills that are titular 'green areas' but in fact are covered by ramshackle and forbidding barrios to La Rinconada, an outlying nucleo housed in sections of a Jesuit elementary school and a nearby windswept hippodrome. My first encounter in the school is with a group of two year-olds and their parents, the exercises of which are the originals of those I saw in Raploch: a Spanish version of 'The Itsy Bitsy Spider', complete with gestures, rhythm play with tambourine and sticks, plastic egg rattles constituting a first experience of orchestral ensemble, games with pitch and movement. Very sweet here, as it was very sweet there. The second is a group of three to five year-olds who have been together less than a year, sitting at smiling attention on tiny plastic chairs in a small blue-painted room, dark hair, dark eyes glistening, quarter-sized violins under their arms. They begin and the sheer force of their sing-song chants, the applications of their bows on open strings pushes me back against the concrete wall, my eyes shot with tears. I feel myself tumbling through the looking glass into another world or at least dimension *into conversion?*

I have experienced these same exercises in Raploch and Lambeth, have observed early string lessons in Ramallah and will again in Tower Hamlets and Islington, London, but this energy is something totally other, this confident commitment, this joy in the doing and the giving, this quality of sound. Even at this early stage the teachers, who are products of El Sistema themselves and therefore of the same or similar communities in which they teach, are demanding excellence from their charges, knowing that they are fully capable of delivering and the children know this as well. They see this in surrounding examples, in their teachers, the older students who are always sharing what they know, so nine year-olds assist six year-olds, a twelve year-old trumpeter who has mastered complex notation and transposition instructs his slightly older classmates though they produce surer sounds in the upper register, fifteen year olds are willing desk mates to aspiring ten year-olds; and they see excellence within themselves. If they don't achieve excellence this time they will the next or the next or the next. They won't be chastised or humiliated as long as they give their all. In the meantime they are contributing, are part of a joyous whole and love is all around them, in touch, in verbal counsel as well as in the notes permeating the air, the palpable keystone of all we survey.

The wonders of this land are replete at every turn: At an early evening performance of Mahler's Second Symphony by a youthful Caracas-based orchestra for representatives of El Sistema's Andean Conference, that is Colombia, Bolivia, Ecuador, Peru, Panama, Brazil all of which have Sistema programs in varying degrees of development: toddlers in their mothers' laps with perhaps siblings among those playing, not fidgeting, whining or vocalizing in any way, paying rapt attention all the way through. The vast majority of the audience appear to be working class and all familiar with the arcane concert etiquette of when and when not to applaud. I am captivated by the female soloists waiting serenely for their cues in their inexpensive formal gowns of mint green and daffodil yellow. The mezzo's face is so indigenous in aspect that it invites comparison to a Mayan frieze; her hooding eyelids are painted bright emerald green. Her voice is fervent and pure when her time comes, her slender frame totally inhabited by man's greatest need to be in heaven and her determination to return to God. *I am on the path of which she sings. I can feel it under my feet. Rapture.*

In an impoverished corner of the Miranda state city of

Guarenos, three and four year-olds sprawl on the floor of a reclaimed police station, copying musical notation into exercise books, reading music before they can do the same in Spanish. It is only here that I see the peak of poverty on young cheeks and slender torsos. Which renders the animating glow imparted eyes by these lessons all the more heartening. Older children practicing in any available space are without this peak. Spiritual nourishment within the grasps of these fragile shoots, with physical strengthening at its side?

With side-worn baseball caps, treasured 'kicks' and mock-machismo sparring about their abilities to shine, working class teenage boys who having gone a different way might be menacing the streets, find their cool in the mastery of intricate music with their mates. This cool, their cool is without the studious aloofness, the abhorrence of mistakes, the refusal to invest in anything other than what it takes to maintain the pose that I've seen, occasionally jousted with, in other impoverished environments. I can't help but celebrate it as an alternative example to the gangster masque that has captivated dispossessed youth around the globe.

A chill and rainy day at Jordan High School South Central Los Angeles in the early 1990s. I have been asked to take on the boys from the group that was established to duplicate the efforts with a girls' group that I formed two years before. Gang membership is a fact of life in this school and the streets that surround it. The abiding philosophy is respect and its violation is paid in blood. We discuss what definition of respect demands a fight to the death at the inadvertent stumble over someone's shoes. Their eyes are young, wanting to communicate despite their indifferent slouches against the walls. Hence the necessity of low-pulled brims. Vulnerabilities cannot be revealed. Discovery is too physically and emotionally dangerous. Too many children dying then and continuing to die. Children I spoke to. How many of whom might have been saved if musical instruments had been as plentiful and as easily attainable as guns and knives? Had been guided into their hands rather

*than guns and knives? How many would have declared, explored and tested
their humanity, satisfied their adolescent penchant towards risk, with music
as their medium rather than blood?*

I am taken to the former youth detention facility of Los
Chorros, amid dusty trees, chipped paint, thin and docile dogs,
next to the fourth most dangerous barrio in the country. The
Los Chorros nucleo caters to 4,000 children under the direction of clarinetist Lennar Acosta, arresting knife scar snaking
about his jaw eloquent testimony to the fate he escaped,
recently returned from year in Bonn as apprentice to one of
the world's premier organ manufacturers where he was an integral member of the team responsible for Fundamusical's new
organ in its breath-taking new Caracas headquarters. A six
year-old girl arrives on her father's flimsy motor bike, pink
helmet secured under her chin, violin strapped to her back. In
addition to music instruction, the nucleo boasts the only wind
and brass instrument-making and repair facility in this part of
the continent, open to any member of the community serious
about learning, making do with minimum equipment and
much determination.

I am sharing my visit with representatives of the
Liechtenstein-based Hilti Foundation, one of Fundamusical's
most generous supporters beyond the Venezuelan government. The Hilti Foundation's parent group has a number of
activities but its most important is the manufacture of all
manner of heavy tools. The Hilti men among us have been
appropriately attentive during miscellaneous musical performances but in the instrument repair workshop their concentration escalates exponentially; they are in their element, observing closely, critically, fingering implements, asking questions.
The workshop has but one lathe bought second hand at the
'great expense' of nearly $10,000. It has many of the innu-
merable forms, collets, tubes and wedges needed for its many

tasks but not all. They too can be 'very expensive' when and if they can be found.

'How expensive?' asks one of the Hilti men.

'As much as $100 for one form,' comes the answer.

I manage to control the edges of my mouth while blessing any power that is for my privileged good fortune. $100 is of course as peanuts to the Hiltis. Before our group takes its leave a pledge has been given for a second lathe and complete complement of the necessary for any instrument bound for this site. Satisfaction abounds for both the givers and receivers of the directed bounty.

Throughout our time at Los Chorros the sweet Josea is always at our side. A Down's Syndrome boy of perhaps fourteen, Josea shadows Lennar wherever Lennar goes, carrying camera tripods to make himself useful, but at each ensemble performance he stands close to whoever is conductor, conducting himself, on tempo perhaps 75 per cent of the time and distracting no one, annoying no one. With no social net of any kind beyond modest unemployment compensation payments available, the welfare of disabled children is a major worry for working parents but they are welcome in Fundamusical. Josea is as much a part of Los Chorros as the young conductor leading the nucleo's highest level band through a spine-tingling rehearsal of Tchaikovsky's Slavonic Dances.

In Barquisimeto, capital city of the inland state of Lara and birthplace of Gustavo Dudamel and where José Antonio Abreu grew to maturity, Fundamusical operates a Special Education center where variously disabled young people participate in choirs and bands of the highest quality. Again with the Hilti group in Caracas I attend a special concert performed by its White Glove Choir composed of the deaf, the hearing, the autistic and learning disabled signing in flowing rhythm with a companion vocal choir piercing the heart. After performance the children circulate, greet and hug. The Hiltis are receiving scrolls and small white gloves in presentation boxes. I hold back for I'm an observer not a benefactor, but the children will have none of it. I receive white gloves and whisper *'Kömmen die Tränen'* to the Hilti woman by my side. She nods and we are joined by the flow of our tears.

Along with its motto *Tocar y Luchar*, To Play and To Fight, Fundamusical is pledged to take everyone who comes to its doors and make do however they can. Though some will be brought at age two and three, others are equally welcome to enter in their teens, so now, after thirty-seven years in 286 nucleos, some 5,400 teachers and 2,200 auxiliary personnel currently servicing close to 400,000 young people, 90 per cent of whom are from low socio-economic backgrounds, with a goal of 1,000,000 for 2020 in a country whose population is less than 26,000,000.

Stories upon stories, images upon images, music above all and all suffused with love. Wondrous.

Twentieth century notions of cultural identity with their concentration on ethnic, racial and religious delineations are inadequate before the possibilities and challenges of El Sistema. The breadth and success of Fundamusical's transformative exemplar demand that instead we prise open our rote and lazy attitudes about identity to encompass man's intrinsic, global humanity and its burgeoning capacities. As is the essential reality of many countries, the problems instigating José Antonio Abreu's intervention in Venezuela were and are those of class, a poverty of opportunities for a major portion of its people with consequent disaffection and crime; but unlike other Northern countries now exploring home-grown transplant of El Sistema, Venezuela had no network of social welfare charged with underpinning the survival of the country's less fortunate and thus no tradition of entitlement among

Abreu's target population. There is no expectation that some
Other could be relied upon to provide the necessities of life
and, according to an unscientific survey among those I
encountered, no particular grudges against this Other as well.
Also in this mix is a state educational system that has been
middling at best. It is not uncommon among the less fortunate
for children to abandon school at age eight or nine, sometimes
because they are needed to augment the family income, sometimes simply because they are bored. There was and is however a pervasive desire among Venezuelans for self-betterment,
an openness to new possibilities and, save for members of a
very small elite, the understanding that making any personal
progress, rising any extra steps, will not be easy, will take a
tremendous amount of time and effort, must be fought for in
fact. Fundamusical's charge of course is to redefine the notion
of 'fight', to redirect its charges away from the surrounding
tendencies towards physical violence into one of communal,
artistic mastery and spiritual fulfilment, to fight and play for
life, believing that even very young children can and will fight
hard for this ideal.

The hours devoted to this fight are long — for children
from the age of six or seven depending on their stage of
development, three hours or more a day, six days a week —
child time that in many other countries is only given to team
or elite sports training and therefore the province of those
designated few considered to have or a being urged toward
special talents. That Venezuelans have embraced El Sistema is
very much a consequence of their cultural and very elastic attitudes towards time as well as their confidence in the capacities
of children, including the very young. That El Sistema participants are willing to spend additional hours getting something
right, taking advantage of the visit of anyone with something
to teach them by pushing back or aside other appointments if

need be, bespeaks a culture where time isn't apportioned into dictatorial increments and punctuality is neither deified or even expected, i.e. not that of many Northern societies where assiduous time management is both a prerequisite for economic advancement and an indication of one's ability to take part in such a quest in a recent parlance being 'ready for prime time'.

As the Civil Rights Movement became momentous, American Negroes spoke of being 'ready', ready for integration, later ready for revolution: in other words leaving behind Colored People's Time, being late, maybe not showing up at all, a strategy for those with minimum control of their destiny. CPT, a term used with both affection and derision, often at the same time. Why bow to the oppressor's dominion including his obsession with the ticking of clocks? Instead this small defiance that became habit, and caricature. The Temptations, Curtis Mayfield and thus we sang of being 'ready'. Though lyrics might also be speaking of relationships the idea of being ready, to be a worthy participant in the dominant culture/economy. Accepted now, adopted now by competitive Northern-based people originally from other climes.

During my time in Caracas many Abreu fellows spoke of the challenges of establishing U.S. nucleos without this time flexibility. With schools, parents and children themselves accustomed to strictly measured increments of time and culturally imprinted towards increasingly short attention spans, wanting quantifiable results within these short spans, how to inculcate El Sistema values and harvest El Sistema results?

And this development of the unscreened very young. Their inclusion in El Sistema was instituted in the early 1990's by conductor and violinist Susan Siman, one of Fundamusical's earliest and most dynamic teachers and now director of a Sistema-based youth orchestra under the auspices of the Miami Symphony. Siman was responding to parents, in this land without nursery schools, wanting similar stimulation and care for their very young children as that on offer for older siblings, as well as her own desire to see if this could be accomplished. The first intake group was one hundred and twenty, some as young as two years old, many still in diapers and with parents in attendance as both potty and teaching assistants. (The inclusion of parents from the earliest stages of their children's involvement in the System is an integral element in Fundamusical's charge toward cohesive community. At all nucleos parents are present in abundance, often demonstrating their commitment to their children's participation by constructing life-size paper models of the string instruments they have chosen to play. This practice has been adopted by Raploch's Big Noise. The children familiarize themselves with hand positions, postures and care with the models so as to treat the real thing with requisite tenderness and on my visit a fairly young and tattooed father of five spoke of making these models with tender pride.) In less than one year, Siman's experimental pre-school group was performing a version of Vivaldi. Again wondrous, but for these Venezuelan children in the context of a community where music and music study is all around, with a leader with the empathetic charisma and skill of Susan Siman and excellence as the standard even for tiny mites, believable wonder. That the programs I first observed outside of Venezuela were not progressing so rapidly points first and foremost to the fact that they are very new and feeling their way towards the establishment of a new culture in the schools and communities in which they are based. The System had after all been up and functioning for almost twenty years when Siman initiated her program, had already gone through its own teething problems such as convincing the boys in thrall to a narrow definition of *machismo* that string-playing was indeed something done by 'real men', and was surrounded by belief in what it could achieve; but I feel that it is telling that upon their visit to Raploch's Big Noise in November 2009, the parting comments from members of the SBYO's Millennium String

Quartet after a short and joy-filled residency were 'You can push them harder you know.'

It is almost inevitable that programs that seek to instill a new or simply different approach to any number of things: religion, hygiene, education, music, will be depending on the missionary impulse in their early incarnations, well-intentioned outsiders entering an environment foreign to their own hoping to share/impart their version of the light. A complex wire walk this, with many far from impressive historical examples of cultural insensitivity if not downright imperialism and many more subject to continuous debate. Though I have often found myself on the side of the questioners I'd be dishonest to dismiss this impulse out of hand.

In 1881, two white Christian ladies from Massachusetts travelled to Atlanta, Georgia to establish the Atlanta Baptist Female Seminary in the basement of a local African-American church. My great-great grandmother was among the thirteen ex-slave women who constituted what would three years hence become Spelman College's first graduating class. Three further female generations of my family continued that tradition and indeed before the widespread integration of white institutes of higher learning in the twentieth century's latter decades the vast majority of African-American college graduates came from schools established by nerves-of-steel Northern missionaries travelling into the war-ravaged and often hostile South after the American Civil War. I may argue with some of their philosophies and manifestations of same, but the overall effect — the training of the vast majority of teachers, doctors and other professionals who serviced the African-American community during the century following Emancipation — must be recognized as to the good. For obvious reasons of the education and cultural orientations of their earlier lives, the vast majority of those who have come to teach in the music education programs I have visited, both the El Sistema offshoots, those of independent development but similar intent, and Al Kamandjâti, are young, white, middle class, often the products of more lenient upbringings than the norm of their new locations and dedicated to neither acting nor appearing culturally insensitive to both students and parents.

Gradual process with continuous gently upbeat encouragement tends to be their mean, with excellence either redefined or configured as a somewhere-out-there goal beyond pleasure dome. In the United Kingdom *noli tangere* protocols have become the norm and are making inroads in the United States: do not touch let alone embrace any child not related to you by blood or allowed by parental intercession. Do not bodily impede the progress of an unrelated-to-you child hell-bent on connecting with oncoming traffic, rather stand by and watch in non-paedophilic innocence. Do not approach and gently question a toddler who appears to be all alone in a park, this last implied by a recent advertised appeal by the U.K.'s National Society for the Prevention of Cruelty to Children with the largest print reserved for the questions 'Should I just mind my own business?' 'Should I do something?' These rules and attendant anxieties combined for some with a natural reticence can reinforce cultural distances between teacher and students. Venezuela is an extremely tactile society and supportive, embracing touch is a basic ingredient of its nucleo culture. One can't expect willy-nilly touch from those neither raised nor inclined in that way but to approach results akin to those in Venezuela an emotional touch, an emotionally palpable laying-on of hands despite any sort of distancing difference is an absolute necessity for bridging such distances and establishing trust.

In thirty-seven years Fundamusical has produced continuous waves of home-grown teachers, teachers who have come from the self-same communities or at least environments as their charges, whose connections of blood and experience are such that they convey subliminally as well as through example, touch and exhortation that excellence is both desirable and attainable. They expect it in their charges as they experienced it themselves and there is nothing tentative in either their approach or their belief.

A few months after Caracas I speak to an English music programmer about the El Sistema USA conference I was unable to attend. She tells me of a demonstration rehearsal in which Gustavo Dudamel led members of the Youth Orchestra of Los Angeles (YOLA) aged eight through twelve through a portion of Mahler's First Symphony, gently but firmly demanding that the children repeat and repeat and repeat a very few bars, not leading them further until he felt real progress had been made. The impassioned reaction of this woman, whom I greatly respect: 'But they were just young!' To which I responded, 'But that's the essence of El Sistema, don't you see? The difference between there and here. You think they're too young to work that hard. He knows that they can do it and will both thrive and love it when they do.' I didn't at all think her reaction infected by thoughts toward color and class, rather a different notion of both what should be asked of children and what they are capable of.

Dudamel's success with the children of YOLA is undoubtedly aided by, in addition to his charismatic celebrity, his being so much 'like them'. More difficult for outsiders to engender similar trust, especially if they are harboring any doubts, about the place, in the mission or more fundamentally in themselves but not impossible, particularly with the adoption of what arts learning consultant and Senior Advisor to El Sistema USA Eric Booth calls one of 'El Sistema's Open Secrets.' Most important of these Booth describes as 'loving children into wholeness'; for it is the happiness of its participants, the aura of love that surrounds and emanates from them, that is at least as striking in any nucleo as the beauty of its sounds; and love of course gives no thought to arbitrary differences.

Not easy perhaps for those whose own musical training has been tainted if not characterized by castigation and stress, the metaphorical if not physical rulers slapped on uncertain, 'lazy' fingers, minds and backs, not wanting to duplicate the lessons of their youth but carrying unfortunate imprints in their senses' memories. In their undertaking of this road this new generation and style of music teaching is declaring its independence from old patterns, but with no magic wands available overnight change can't be expected and a constant self-assessment must be one of their essential tools. That all children embrace what is offered to them in love, those whose lives have been characterized by chaos and disappointment in equal measure to those whose lives have been untainted by care, is a basic truism of our species, but to cultivate a new way in grounds blighted with gnarled roots and constipated traditions will take courage, tenacity (no doubt occasionally accompanied by tears) and, depending on circumstance, a generous dose of realpolitik in addition to lofty intent. At the end, however, so many blessings.

In autumn 2010 Fundamusical's younger youth orchestra, the Teresa Carreño — named for the nineteenth century Venezuelan pianist who both conquered and scandalized more than one continent — embarked on its first European tour and international debut: Bonn, Vienna, Berlin, Amsterdam, Madrid, ending with two performances in London where Fundamusical has had a special champion in the Southbank Centre's former Head of Music Marshall Marcus who taught strings for more than a year during the System's earliest manifestation. For all the accolades bestowed on the Simón Bolivar

Youth Orchestra, during its triumphal progression in the spring of 2009 there had been attendant grumbles that some of its members were pushing thirty years old, a bit long in the tooth to be classified as youthful. Were they the only manifestation of this 'miracle', its only musicians up to the world's withering gaze? With the Teresa Carreño's 160 members between the ages of fourteen and twenty-one displaying blistering technical facility, musicality and passion at every turn the answer was a thundering '¡No!'

Again I am captivated by their colors, the lush fawns, marronys and copper of the girls' naked arms, the dark lustrous hair, but this is as nothing compared to their music's inspired precision. There are more female section heads than in the SBYO or in any other orchestra that I have seen: two of the three rotating leaders, the second violins, the oboes, flutes and bassoons, and they do the job; they more than do the job. A set of Fives: the Beethoven, the Prokofiev and a Tchaikovsky Fifth that ripped the roof from the orchestra hall. Tchaikovsky is a Venezuelan favorite and prominent among the composers whose large sinuous sounds are the meat of a system that concentrates on the beauty and strength of the large ensemble, but for me his Fifth had become the stuff of easy listening muzak, the scoring for all kinds of low-rent television offers, no bones, muzzled in toffee. The Teresa Carreñoniños showed me different: articulate dynamism, heart-rending passion and so much love, joy, glory in the delivery. I was converted yet again, and again the radiant humility lashed with teenage exuberance of the players applauding their standing soloists more fervently than the standing audience. Happy for them, happy for themselves and in themselves, happy for Venezuela, happy for being able to give, happy to clown and dance through the Latinate encores, blazing beacons for all those in need of light. *Such an extraordinary public relations coup for a land riven with domestic conflict and not best loved by many in the West. The brilliant red, yellow and blue of the jackets donned for the encores and then tossed into the crowd, the country spelled out in white across the back unmissable with the conductor at his work: V-E-N-E-Z-U-E-L-A. The waving flags, the joyous smiles and fears of quixotic left-wing dictatorship, anti-Western alliances banished perhaps for longer than the present moment by this gamboling excellence, these benevolent, beautiful and talented young people.*

The Teresa Carreño's visit to London was followed not long after by the sixty member strong Venezuelan Brass Ensemble established in 2003 by Thomas Clamor, a Colleague of the Berlin Philharmonic trumpet section until the seductive power of doing such good, being welcomed as family and becoming so integral a part of so redemptive a mission convinced Clamor to resign from that orchestra and devote himself more completely to both Fundamusical in Venezuela and the establishment of what he hopes to be a brass beginning on his own side of the water. (At this writing Clamor's European Brass Ensemble contains young members from ten EU states based somewhat appropriately at the Austrian Benedictine monastery of Melk.) The quality of the Venezuelan playing was as ever superb, culminating before the interval with a virtuosic brass arrangement of Mussorgsky's Pictures at an Exhibition. The second half of the concert was far more Latin in flavor — and more fundamentally crowd-pleasing for a sold-out crowd looking to be warmed by Latin fire on that wintry northern night — but I found myself especially struck by the Ensemble's last encore, the musical joke of Johann Strauss' 'Perpetuum Mobile'. As the players and their conductor scampered about the stage into the wings and back again in a manner far more Germanic than Latin with broad, genuine smiles I thought this their happily loving tribute to their founder from Berlin as well as amusing and sincere testimony to the plasticity of cultural boundaries and exchange.

* * *

There are those who question the futures of Fundamusical's progeny. Even with a goal of 1,000,000 participants by 2020 in Venezuela and whatever may develop in the Andean Conference there won't be teaching positions for all who emerge, so what will all these musicians be doing? But such questions are missing the point. El Sistema is not in the business of turning out professional musicians with an eye towards global conquest; that seems to me more a Far Eastern purview *pace* the millions of young Chinese being trained with goals of becoming the next Lang Lang or violinist Chen Xi, a good number of whom have formed a steady flow into elite Western conservatories and orchestras, displaying the same attention to technical brilliance that has characterized Chinese forays into the sports of gymnastics and diving (though often, it would seem without the joy attendant to the El Sistema experience). With their increasing international exposure undoubtedly a number of Fundamusical graduates will make their way into orchestras outside of Latin America; one can only wait and see what effect the exponential increase in El Sistema's renown will have on its own culture; but the System's purpose and emphasis has always been to develop whole, enriched human beings who are happy parts of a holistic community whatever their eventual roles or jobs may be whether or not playing an instrument remains an integral part of their lives. With its emphasis on the ensemble El Sistema also promotes and produces a form of collective joy that has become increasingly rare in the moneyed, digitized North, one in which the participants do rather than observe or virtualize. Sistema students feel themselves part of a living, singing, dancing whole, not isolated pods whose means of expression are little more than manipulating the vicarious experiences to which they have access and the purchase of things that they haven't made. Through them we are reminded of fundamental aspects of human character and identity that have become all too rare in our race towards accumulation and prominence.

'I feel like the doors of heaven have opened up.'
Adam Hart, 12 year-old African-American member of the
Youth Orchestra of Los Angeles

Young Adam's isn't the only heart-warming early testimony to the benefits and promise of El Sistema's first excursions outside of Venezuela. Visual record and its distribution are easy these days and there is enough media interest in young children of difficult backgrounds improving their lives via music that internet searches of same garner plentiful rewards, which is not to say that there hasn't been resistance. In January 2011 the New England Conservatory announced that it would be severing its identification with El Sistema USA because the expansion plans of ES USA were incompatible with the Conservatory's fundamental mission. Though differences between the two were quietly resolved, two months later that development prompted Executive Director of New York City's Center for Arts Education Richard Kessler to state that 'El Sistema as it is in Venezuela will never happen in the United States… Our Government does not fund the arts on that kind of level, on that sort of basis. So what happens is El Sistema has to be translated into something that's American and I think in the translation, generally speaking, it doesn't look very different than the many very good youth orchestra programs.' However, as has been frequently attested by many with the experience of both traditional musical training and conservatories on the one hand and Fundamusical on the other, with their first priority being social change rather than musical prowess, El Sistema nucleos are very different from traditional youth orchestras both in template and in aspiration. Should the El Sistema model be successful beyond Latin America, it is capable of upending musical status quos in whatever Northern country it takes root and thus any number of current notions of what a musician and most particularly a classical musician is. Is he or she a member of an elite or the *hoi polloi*? In spirit is western classical music more of Dionysius or Apollo? Where is this music offered and received? How and by whom? Unsettling for some, especially perhaps those with eroding territories to protect, for this is nothing less than the dawning of a new paradigm.

In January 2008 after a good ten months in service to the election of Barack Obama I turned up in New Hampshire a week before its primary to do whatever it was I could. Two days after my arrival Obama won the Iowa caucus. I was exhilarated by our win. How could I not be? We'd proven the naysayers wrong. The campaign's grass roots organizing had borne giddily bounteous fruit; and, against speculations of folk telling pollsters one thing in order to appear anti-racist but actually doing the exact opposite, White People had voted for the Black Guy. All over the country a huge number of African-Americans had been waiting for just such evidence that a vote for Barack Obama would not be one tossed into the mud; they could see that Barack Obama was really a contender in this race; but then it all got too crazy. The polls and indeed the Clinton campaign itself seemed to indicate an implosion of the much-vaunted most powerful, well-funded and well-organized political machine of the modern era. This was wrong. The Obama campaign accomplished an amazing feat coming from a 25-point deficit in November 2007 to losing by just two points in New Hampshire on January 8th the following year, but after the headiness of the five days between Iowa and chilly New England this felt a reversal, when better characterization might have been market correction. It was of this correction that a very hoarse and tired but, as ever, inspirational (and funny) Barack Obama spoke at a Boston fundraising lunch I was privileged to attend the very next day.

All the expectations and palaver had had him feeling like Icarus, he said. He'd been flying too high too soon. 'Everybody believed I'd win. Hell, I believed it myself… but this feels more right.' The crux of his message: that we'd always known that the status quo wasn't going to just roll over and play dead. Of course they would fight, hard, to hold onto their power and they did; and they still do.

One would hope that the possibilities of El Sistema will have fewer problems in the rocky new soils in which it's now being sown than the presidency of Barack Obama but it too is an evolutionary change and only time will tell. In the meantime the Abreu Fellows do their work.

I spoke to and was impressed by all of the Fellows that I met in Caracas but I am a beast with habits and so was particularly intrigued by the two in their number who are black, Stanford Thompson a Curtis Institute-trained trumpet player originally from Decatur, Georgia but pledged to establishing a nucleo in Philadelphia; and Dantes Rameau, a Canadian bassoonist of Haitian and Cameroonian parents heading to the former Allen family seat of Atlanta, Georgia. They are achingly young, barely in their mid-20s but witheringly intelligent and determinedly focused. I follow the progress of their programs on Facebook, Philadelphia's Play On, Philly! and the Atlanta Music Project and skype them one year on for a brief update, for this is the twenty-first century and simple telephoning the stuff of dinosaurs.

Their programs have started modestly: an initial eighty in Philadelphia and what got whittled down to twenty in Atlanta. (After his years at the Curtis Institute Stan already had a local musically sympathetic network more in place, while Dantes was a very recent transplant and had less than two months to introduce himself to Atlanta and potential students as well as getting the program up and running.) With an immediate intent to form orchestras rather than just string ensembles, both programs offer a large range of instruments even to those children still in possession of baby teeth. In both programs some 95+ per cent of the children are black and three-quarters are eligible for free school lunches, the traditional indicator of family need. While Stan mentioned with complete discretion that other of his colleagues had experienced some parental resistance in the early stages, i.e. 'who are you [white person] to be telling me what's good for my [black] child' as one might expect this hasn't been a daunting challenge for either Dantes or himself. (Dantes' aside: 'They don't really figure that I'm from someplace else. I'm just black.')

As well as the target student demographic, the city councils of both Atlanta and Philadelphia reflect the predominantly black racial make-up of their populations as well as the white and middle-class black flight to surrounding suburbs, with the consequent drastic decline in the tax base from which educational funding is gleaned. Both young men have been greeted with sympathetic political reception if not in these financially straitened times as much funding as one might wish (though hardly these days expect), but it is their own example and drive which is propelling their programs. While both come from middle class backgrounds and neither were tempted by the street, the steel necessary to choose and excel in classical music as lone black wolves in predominantly white packs is clearly evident in their characters and in their leadership. Both have come from disciplined upbringings and have no problem with the El Sistema mantra of excellence as well as joy. 'I don't do cute' was Stan's reply to my question about what music the children were learning. 'They are learning classical music in accepted progression.' After the resolution of early disciplinary challenges that came with not being used to sticking with one thing Dantes says his kids 'start to enjoy their development'. Both speak of long-term commitments, Stan with a view to picking up the ball being dropped by all the education and arts funding cuts and establishing a whole culture of community nucleos staffed increasingly with student mentors teaching younger students and orchestras designed to bring joy and focus into communities where these elements have become frequent or complete strangers.

Race is not the only determinate in play. Even in America class is at least as important a hurdle to overcome. The mixed-race founder and director of the Sphinx Foundation Aaron Dworkin was adopted as a baby by a secular Jewish couple and grew up on New York City's Upper West Side. Dworkin's determined mission is to get more minority string players into orchestras, a task involving a far more middle class component than most El Sistema initiatives, but for the Foundation's outreach programs in the hard streets of Detroit and Flint, Michigan the tall, brown-skinned Dworkin told me that white instructors from similar circumstances are often far more effective in reaching the kids than he is. Dan Trahey, the charismatic white leader of Baltimore's OrchKids program, is a case in point. Trahey selected to play trombone because it was the last instrument left in the cupboard that his school would allow him to borrow and train on for free when it was his time to choose. The fact that he learned to love it was pure chance, but his ability to empathize with his charges is not. In every case however the real determinant is long-term and essentially selfless commitment, the commitments of their lifetimes; for which time will tell.

So again our question: Are we listening? As we seek a new

campground along a new way, as we Endeavour to inspire the vulnerable and heal ourselves.

Yes, yes, we are.

'Neither silence nor stillness last...'

13

'Change is the only certainty…'

Al Kamandjâti brochure

Time passes as I peruse my notes and parse my words, events hurtling onward even faster than usual in this quicksilver century, in North Africa and the Middle East most particularly. While Palestine has not been as overtly engulfed as its news-dominating neighbors I suspect that it can't be unaffected. With all the new nation-building swirling about I ask myself if Al Kamandjâti and its students are maintaining the ecumenical stance towards music I had deduced one year before. I want to be at an end but am ill at ease completing this consideration without a return however briefly to learn what I can, to reassess if necessary. It is brief, one week in June 2011.

I take the same flight on the same budget airline to Tel Aviv as before, but it is completely different in character. This time passengers are the mix I'd originally expected of tourists, students, family travelling back or forth. All are subdued; there is no village atmosphere. I didn't imagine what I experienced fourteen months before but it's feeling a trifle through-the-looking-glass. *And this shade of regret, as though I'm missing it, the energy, even tumult? Easy for me in my secure, untrammeled life to fancy the challenge of that she-monster.*

I take the same route to Ramallah: the shuttle to East Jerusalem, the ramshackle bus across the Qalandia checkpoint, past still open produce markets, into the town. It is late but I know where I'm going this time and can even advise a back-packing German student, who hopes to sofa surf in Ramallah as he did in Cairo and Ethiopia. A jive-talking slip of a young

American Arab from Chicago takes Philip under his wing.
Recently married to a Palestinian girl he can't bring Philip into
her family's home but will call a few bro's. 'There's ghetto
everywhere, my friend. A man got to hustle.' Philip is interested in music and wants to spend two or three weeks doing his
bit for the Palestinian cause. I invite him to drop by Al
Kamandjâti. I will never see him again and suspect he finds a
different adventure than what first he sought, but he is robust,
has already travelled far and Ramallah's crime rate is still low.
He will survive. I choose to walk the short way to my hotel this
time rather than wait for a cab. I almost miss my street because
the major hub from which it radiates has been annihilated for
resurfacing. Sidewalks no longer exist. My luggage wheels are
worried by sand and rubble; cars are bouncing cautiously
through crevice and debris. Several are expensive. Even in the
dark I can sense a further state of becoming.

The next morning I find my way to Al Kamandjâti without
hitch. The sun is bright but the temperature moderate. The
hills of Ramallah have traditionally been a refuge from
summer heat and despite all the construction and ever-increasing traffic, with the near continuous breezes pollution is not
yet a problem. The Kamandjâti courtyard is as welcoming as
before and, by mid-morning, already bustling with various
musicians and two film crews. It had been February when I
was here last, a quiet time in the school's calendar: no concerts
only the day-to-day charge and challenge of lessons and
rehearsal; but I've arrived in the midst of its sixth annual Music
Days Festival, two weeks during which Al Kamandjâti students
and teachers together with musicians from Europe and
America perform both Oriental and Western music all over the
West Bank in a variety of shape-shifting ensembles. Access to
Gaza had been desired but ultimately deemed too delicate,
indeed possibly volatile, a time by the French, who are arbiters

of most non-military and Palestinian entry. The Western musicians play the role taken by older students in El Sistema, shoring up the sound of the various ensembles and coaching, individually or in sections, the Kamandjâti students who are taking part. Many of the professionals have returned year after year, often performing in AK's December Baroque music festival as well, and they have eager pupils in the dozens of AK students participating in these Days who are spending Venezuelan amounts of time with their instruments and the making of music. They are the majority of Kamandjâti's most dedicated participants and they are an impressive bunch. Among them:

Mahmoud, now 18, of the effervescent smile and the blistering technique, who will be off for further violin studies at the conservatoire in Toulouse come September with a stipend from the French consulate in Palestine.

Yannel, a 19 year-old percussionist from Jenin who first saw an AK ensemble perform four years before and knew that this was for him. Come September he too will be on his way to a French conservatoire, in Bordeaux this time with assistance from the Al Qattan Foundation. Yannel feels no cultural barriers between himself and any music. There are simply different techniques: Oriental music primarily hands, Western primarily sticks. He will return to Palestine to teach and perform in both when his studies are complete.

As will Ala, a thirteen year-old violinist, who has been studying for six years. Ala plays Bach and Beethoven when she's happy and Oriental music when she's sad. Both are integral parts of who she is. Despite the impediments inherent simply in her being Palestinian and wanting that which would be deemed normal in most parts of the world, Ala knows that she will achieve her dream and she'll be playing a violin that her brother has made. Shehadah is currently training to become Kamandjâti's resident luthier and the tailpiece of his sister's instrument will be honed from wood of Palestine.

Majd, who is writing his first concerto for trombone and orchestra at 16 after four years of study and whom I see taking his first steps in learning jazz changes.

Rashed, a tall and ebullient violinist of twelve who loves Vivaldi above all with Bach a close second and whose dazzling command of English is the result of seven years study in school enhanced by his parallel enthusiasms for The Simpsons and teen horror flicks. Rashed also rates physics and basketball very highly. Rashed too lives in Jenin, but after playing duties there makes the two-hour journey down to Ramallah every day during this time with his violin-playing buddy Najir.

Laila, a shy and thoughtful cellist of fourteen who has been studying four years and shares Rashed's interest in physics. Laila finds Oriental music easier to understand because of who and where she is, but both it and Western classical music are secure in her heart. She loves both, is dedicated to both.

I hear of twelve year-old Fadi who with the Jenin Oriental Ensemble sings traditional and popular Arabic material but is also developing an Italian baroque concert repertoire featuring Scarlati, Bononcini and Caldara, chomping at the bit for Verdi and wants to be the Palestinian Pavarotti because Pavarotti is whom he's heard of.

Most of the children also voice an appreciation of Palestinian hip hop. To Majd it's 'a very creative way of delivering a message about the Palestinian cause to the whole world.' Laila 'also likes to hear hip hop [in addition to classical music] because it express[es] our feelings as Palestinians.' So then, following the general youthful trend of not allowing pursuit of one music to disallow ownership of another.

Again, as is my wont, not a scientific sample, but enough that I'm feeling that Al Kamandjâti's inclusive approach to music hasn't altered in this new period of Arab awakening but neither has the long game through which it is being guided by its ever clear-eyed and steadfast founder Ramzi Aburedwan. In the year since my last visit, Ramzi tells me, Kamandjâti has been becoming a stronger presence in both the country and its local communities with warmer acknowledgment from the Palestinian Authority that has as yet neither the power nor the finances to do more. Steady progression then towards his goal of Kamandjâti becoming an integral and initiating component in the reconstruction of Palestine's national cultural identity while at the same time demonstrating resistance to the occupation by playing music in and despite the presence of the Wall. Saying 'We will not accept this!' while bringing more and more music into the lives of ordinary Palestinians. Which I have several opportunities to experience.

First back to the village of Deir Gessane, taking a 'service' (pronounced sir-VEECE) minibus this time instead of Kamandjâti's utility van with Julia, my vocal teacher friend, and another American woman who has been shuttling between Israel and the West Bank for several months doing research for a doctorate on music and conflict resolution. The bright yellow-orange of American school buses, by virtue of an arrangement between VW and the Palestinian Authority the 'service' are in far more plentiful supply now than they were when I was last here; providing cheap, continuous day-long transport between the West Bank's many villages and towns and most points in between. Scheduling is visceral to the driver, as is the pervasive seat-of-the-pants regard to road safety, but one gets to places that would takes days on foot. We alight a few meters from the Kamandjâti center in the village where four pubescent girls are waiting to rehearse their songs for the 6pm performance of the Ramallah Oriental Ensemble, clutching their teddy bear-stickered notebooks, intricately strapped sandals and brightly-painted toenails their seasonal embrace of fashion. The songs are Palestinian and, Julia tells me, describe the angst of being refugees 'for them to know, for it's part of who they are though not their day-to-day existence.' Goats graze in the dry season parch outside the window as the girls sing and with their Hiraz-scaled harmonics a sense in me of the absolute appropriateness of this sound to the winding path of the village road, to the arc of the windows, to the curves and dots of Arabic script. *But which comes first? Which chicken? Which egg? Or am I simply guilty of the most commonplace of cultural stereotyping? For all my protestations and desires to the contrary, how different am I from those I disdain?*

What looks to be most of the women and children of the village are in the center's courtyard, seated in the white plastic chairs ubiquitous throughout most southern climes and all the Third World. Unlike their sisters in more cosmopolitan Ramallah, all of the women of Deir Gessanne are in hijab, but the children are dressed with gentle, characteristic flare. *Girl toddlers in pink sandals adorned with Walt Disney's blonde, Barbie-contoured Tinkerbell. Bootleg dvds are sold here in shops, access to the outer world outweighing ethical thoughts on copyright infringement. Are Disney's anodyne princesses wreaking insidious havoc on little girl dreams here in Palestine as they do in so many other parts of the globe as well?* Due to the late arrival of the Ramallah ensemble and the need of two present film crews to compensate for fast diminishing light the concert's start is delayed some forty-five minutes, but despite the presence of so many young children none in the audience are fractious. Slouched against a pepper tree are four young village men in black jeans, knock-off trainers from China and tight t-shirts which display the contours of toned torsos. They have the aspect of many such young men with not enough to do, looking ready for a fight or communal sexual joshing; but here they wait, murmuring quietly amongst themselves, patient. I'm again aware of a very non-First World arrangement with time. Palestinians wait, for the service, for all kinds of permissions, for their nation. They are familiar with waiting, stoic on the surface no matter what dissatisfactions are roiling underneath, conserving energy for survival?

The concert lasts less than forty-five minutes. The Ramallah Oriental Ensemble, consisting of Mahmoud and Ala on violin, Yannel and instructor Ibrahim on percussion, fifteen year-old Bushra on flute and nineteen year-old Oday on vocals haven't had as much time as they would have wished with the four local singers, who are tentative in their delivery; but the audience isn't disappointed. As the young bravos video the performance on their mobile phones I wonder when, if ever, live music came to Deir Gessanne before the arrival of Al Kamandjâti. A very small thing, this concert, but appreciated and worthy of preservation. With darkness falling and there-fore no guarantee that another service will pass through the village on its last lap back to Ramallah, we catch a ride from Khalil Ghnaim, a communications major denied leave to travel to the University of California Los Angeles where he had earned a place for masters study, now working in Kamandjâti's administration. Nerves are high. The musicians are disap-pointed to have been recorded on local television while not performing to their preferred standard, and Khalil is driving a car with yellow Israeli plates rather than the green required for Palestinians. If the IDF stops us for any reason, there could be hell to pay. We return to Ramallah's Old City without incident but drained.

Day two. Another service to the village of Abu Dis. Ramallah lies to the north of Jerusalem and Abu Dis to the south. Not so far as the crow flies, but since Palestinians are denied access through Jerusalem, a goodly journey around with the restraining Wall most of the time in view, covered with defiant graffiti, strewn with uncollected rubbish. We pass massive quarries on our way and groves upon groves of tree stumps on gentle slopes distant from all construction activity, what remains of hundreds of Palestinian olive trees destroyed in the name of Security but more particularly for the destruction of the family economies based for generations on their fruit and attendant collective souls. The highway, financed by USAID, is modern and smooth, my fellow passengers are quiet, my own body seething with hormones triggered by these offenses to nature, to decency. I am new to this. My Palestinian fellow travelers are not. How must they feel? Colored as it is by my African-American struggle, is my anger self-indulgent?

I hadn't had much notice when I went to Germany for the first time. I was working on one of the last doddering efforts among the plethora of international co-productions that cluttered many a cinema from the late 1960s to the early 1980s, films characterized by cushy budgets, big stars — in this case Marlon Brando, George C. Scott, Marthe Keller, John Gielgud — lovely locations, often with a generous helping of Nazis thrown into the mix. They tended to be more about high-flying tax avoidance than cinematic art and were generally nice little earners for all involved. Second assistant directors were not typically taken along on such jaunts but the African-American first assistant that had hired me didn't want to go to NaziLand by himself and finessed MGM into going against form.

At embarkation my German vocabulary consisted of Danke schön and Eidelweiss, courtesy respectively of pop singer Brenda Lee and dear Oscar II from The Sound of Music. I arrived on sets in Berlin with a Berlitz phrase book in my back pocket having managed to order Rührei for my Frühstück and eventually picked up other expressions essential to my trade such as 'Ruhig, bitte!' Quiet, please! (Though I suspect it sounded more like 'Scrambled, please!') and 'Alle Comparsen am Anfang, bitte!' All extras to starting positions, please! The German members of the crew, taken from the elite cadre of film technicians who catered to these international affairs, were at the very least bilingual, speaking English to mono-lingual Americans and Brits and German among themselves, which of course to my untrained ear just sounded like 'German'. Some eighteen months later I worked with many of the same crew members during the short stint on a film that took me to the Schwartzwald with Diane Keaton, but by then I'd done a crash course in German grammar at UCLA and was spending part of my year in Berlin where I shored up my German watching episodes of Tatort, a long-running German cousin of Law and Order, and expertly dubbed American classic films the English dialogue of which was familiar to me; so when the Germans started speaking their language, what before had been an undistinguishable drone was now a symphony of different tones. This one was speaking Bayrisch, this one Schweitzerdeutsch. That guy was from Tirol. Good God, the sächsisch accent on that electrician! Via more familiarity and a modicum of knowledge, a vastly enhanced sense of reality.

This second trip to Palestine is akin to that second German film set. Just as with my ability to discern nuances in pronunciation there, the haze of valiant music amongst olive trees and almond blossoms, limestone hills and IDF patrols, automatic weapons and young, tentative fingers on string fingerboards observed and absorbed during my first trip is now acquiring more focus. And admittedly, in terms of my political self, more militancy.

Just over the Wall from Jerusalem's Mount of Olives, Abu Dis is not a crime-free municipality. Under the second Oslo agreement of 1995 Ramallah is located in an A zone, an area under the titular full civil and security control of the Palestinian Authority (though the Israeli Defence Force can conduct raids for suspected militants at its whim), which includes an attentive and highly praised police force. Abu Dis is in a B zone, that is under PA civil jurisdiction but with Israeli security control. The small resident number of Palestinian police have no uniforms, no weapons, are not allowed by the Israelis to move into the small headquarters with two detention cells recently built them by the Authority and have therefore been helpless against a growing problem of drugs being brought into the village by Israelis over whom they have no jurisdiction, combined with an escalating local vendetta over land rights that has resulted in an unprecedented two murders over a two month period. I'm feeling more tension in Abu Dis than in any of my previous West Bank locations. It isn't officially a refugee camp but it feels more like the refugee camps of my imaginings. That thing is in the air here, that thing I've felt in São Paolo and Kinshasa, Los Angeles and New York. Barely suppressed rage. Veined with despair.

But not in the village's cultural center where, in a dome-ceilinged room up two steep flights of outdoor stairs, some sixty young children patiently await the Ramallah Oriental Ensemble's noon performance with an undercurrent of tentative eagerness. The music goes well this time. Mahmoud regains his habitual grin and singer Oday encourages the youngsters to clap along to the well-known songs they are playing. Some engage happily but others appear completely taken aback, mystified indeed, and one guesses that this may be their very first encounter with live music played at such a level by anyone let alone their own. A young girl of perhaps five has been eyeing me throughout the play. With my height and hair I know myself to be something of an anomaly here. We make eye contact. She is shy but allows a hesitant smile. I encourage her to clap in time to the music, lead her with quiet clapping of my own. She does so softly, intermittently, then stops. This is all so new. My heart aches at her fragility.

The female teachers are exuberant though. All wear hijab, but when midday prayers begin at the mosque across the way they do nothing to curtail the music and merely close windows to muffle the sound. It is all too much for one little boy. He covers his ears, pleas if not too insistently for the music to stop, which percussionist Yannel smilingly refuses. When the music ends many of the girls approach Bushra to kiss and embrace her, to touch her flute, attempt to blow. The flute leads in many of the Ensemble's arrangements and for a young woman, her hair uncovered, to play so confidently in a group of young men is obviously a point of wonder. Bushra encourages their interest with a gentleness well beyond her fifteen years. One can well imagine that other little girls will follow Bushra's example and thereby open themselves to realities beyond Abu Dis.

Back to Ramallah via service, past the slaughtered groves, the rubbish and the Wall, where the Ensemble plays at the Al-Amari refugee camp later that afternoon. Here the children are hip and sassy, not so well organized. This is where Ramzi grew up and Al Kamandjâti has taught here regularly since its inception. The children engage or don't as it suits. They are exuberant and cheeky, without fear and hungry for attention, the similarities between them and black ghetto kids I've encountered over the years many and profound. *What's your name?' It must be the first English phrase they all learn. It is ubiquitous, becomes hilarious. 'What's your name?' 'My name is Candace.' 'Her name is Candace! Her name is Candace!' 'What's your name?' 'My name is Candace.' Their faces are wreathed with smiles, their joyous curiosity infectious. 'Where you from?' 'I'm from America.' 'America! She's from America!' I suspect not so many from America and certainly not looking like me. From France, Germany, Sweden, Britain but not so many from America. 'What's your name?' 'My name is [Rima, Mohammed, Nisreen, Amara, Aboud].' 'What's your name?' 'My name is Candace.' Ubiquitous, hilarious, poignant. Challenging, me to engage, the world to know that they are here.*

Saturday. I've managed to claim the one empty seat in the van used by the Italian film crew shooting a documentary for Al Kamandjâti's tenth anniversary in 2012 who will be spending the day following the Jenin Oriental Ensemble. The van that picks me up at 7am is battered, white and borrowed from UNESCO, so with diplomatic white license plates that will allow us access to a road typically closed to Palestinians, thus rendering our drive-time thirty minutes shorter than the norm. Being *Shabbat* there are almost no yellow license-plated vehicles on the road, but it is a workday for Palestinians, so frustrating to discover the primary motorway to Nablus and Jenin has been arbitrarily closed by the IDF. *A jeep. Two soldiers. Casual, entitled demeanor. Automatic weapons. No reason given. None sought.* Our van is not exempt from this and joins the diverted traffic down far more narrow country roads to enter Nablus from the side. Passing mature olive groves nestled below settlement-encrusted hillsides awash in Mediterranean sun I search for appropriate phraseology for a question that can only be fraught. Rather than 'who owns these groves?' I ask the quadri-lingual Italian driver/producer who lives here in Palestine 'who harvests these trees?' Palestinians do, he tells me, but it's one of the groves plagued by settlement sewage purposely allowed to flow downward among the trees, another habitual ploy to contaminate the soil and humiliate owners away.

The adolescent boys who comprise the Jenin Oriental Ensemble are already in situ when we arrive, distributing drinks, tuning their instruments. They are supervised by Iyad Staiti, with whom I'd conversed the prior year. Iyad's wife is expecting another child at any moment. If there are complications Nicola, our driver will take over responsibility for the boys. As ever in this life regardless of locale, the show must go on. The Jenin ensemble is larger than its Ramallah counterpart: two modern flutes, one reed flute, Rashed, Najir and another boy on violin, a zither, two ouds, two percussion, Fadi on vocals. With their well-scrubbed faces, recent fashionable haircuts, open personalities and lightly muscled physiques they are the incarnation of Boy Band at its most benevolent, paragons of desire for both schoolgirls and their protective parents.

The Yafa Cultural center of the Balata refugee camp outside of Nablus is the first stop of the day. As ever my slowly adapting synapses discharge confusion at the sight of an extensive warren of cement block-constructed buildings rather than tents *and dust and tsetse flies, maybe a camel or two…* As is the case at many of the camps, the center is a United Nations facility and this one includes a good-sized air-conditioned theatre complete with stage lighting and a sound booth. With delays caused by road diversions and set-up time, the hundreds of student girls between the ages of perhaps eleven and fifteen file into their seats an hour later than planned with neither annoyance nor slouch. The Ensemble's cute boys are well-appreciated by this audience especially twelve-year old Fadi, whose clear tenor voice with coquettish gestures of head and hands, whose total comfort in the spotlight bespeaks a Palestinian Michael Jackson in the making. Born in Japan, Fadi bears a passport from that country and so is able to travel with relative ease. Al Jazeera is also filming the performance and it wouldn't surprise me in the least to learn that despite his aspirations toward opera he'd taken a temporary detour into pop. The girls don't squeal and writhe. I doubt such behavior meshes well with the hijab the vast majority of them wear, but Fadi has them grooving. Happiness all around.

As there is in the Women's center of the Nour Shams camp when we arrive ninety minutes late to find some one hundred younger children of both sexes seated on the floor waiting patiently with their teachers beneath gently circulating ceiling fans. There's only time for two numbers here but unlike in Abu Dis, the children of Nour Shams fully engage with the performance, clapping excitedly at the invitation of their teachers and Iyad, crowing out familiar lyrics with ecstatic abandon. Some twenty minutes later we are on our way back to our vans trailing happy smiles and 'what's-your-names?' No resentment that we arrived so late and leave so quickly. Transported by this gift of music. On to the next. *And in the driving craggy unpopulated hills, blue sky with wisps of cirrus cloud, cultivated valleys, the land appearing vast. Yes, perhaps indeed the cradle of God's earthly creation. Limitless, not a small controversial sliver of the globe. Until you come to a checkpoint, glimpse a proprietary sign, cast even the briefest glimpse back into history.*

On 4 April 2011 actor-director Juliano Mer-Khamis was shot five times by a masked gunman meters away from the Freedom Theatre of Jenin which he had founded five years before. The son of Saliba Khamis, a Palestinian Christian who had been a leader of the Israeli Communist Party and an Israeli Jewish mother, dramatist Arna Mer, Juliano considered himself 100 per cent Palestinian and 100 per cent Jewish, but never so Jewish as he was often made to feel during his work in Jenin. The Theatre's innovative techniques and fearless productions, including an Animal Farm that implied that under the wrong circumstances leaders of the *intifada* could mutate into *haram* (unclean) pig oppressors, had earned both the theatre and its founder great love among many in Jenin's refugee community but deep suspicion as well, to the point that Mer-Khamis was often quoted as being grateful for two things from Israel, Avraham Shlonsky's Hebrew translations of Shakespeare and the instinct of continual awareness gleaned from his paratrooper training. He was taking precautions. Obviously not enough.

The assumption has been that his murderers were Palestinian militants wary of the Western influences that the Freedom Theatre represented. To the intermingling of boys and girls, that had been directed towards Al Kamandjâti two years before, the theatre had added irreverent productions of Western derivation. One of the reasons I'd been eager to join the Italians in their coverage of the day was that, in addition to following the Ensemble around the camps, they'd planned to film in Jenin proper, including what they might discover around Freedom Theatre, which had vowed to continue its work. Old footage existed of Ramzi and Juliano in walking conversation. The Italians wanted to return to that place and I wanted to be with them, my film production-honed street antennae on the alert to glean whatever nuance I might in regards to any simmering cultural tensions, then ponder how these tensions might impact the students of Al Kamandjâti and their school's overall mission. It was not to be.

The Jenin Oriental Ensemble is running two hours behind by the time we arrive in Tulkarem for its last performance of the day at the Al Shera'a-Al Yasser Corporation for Re-Education and Development. A very different event this: rather than masses of eager faces, a line of solemn adolescent young men gathered by their equally solemn male teachers? counselors? I'm feeling a more dogmatic religion here. The adults are generous with much needed cold water but far more aloof in their demeanor than the women we've encountered elsewhere. The Ensemble does its best but they are young and tired and hungry and they are getting nothing but quiet scrutiny from their audience. Later I learn that this is more demonstration/audition than the gift that performance can be, with Kamandjâti hoping to attract some of the Corporation lads into their fold. I could read no signs as to the success of this Endeavour or lack of same but perhaps a brief glimmer as to some of the challenges Al Kamandjâti faces in championing the liberating values of living in music.

After a catch-as-catch-can refueling courtesy of Palestinian fast food and vast jugs of Fanta, the boy band is boisterous and cheerful, but there is tension between Iyad and the film's director with much vociferous Italian and Arabic back and forth. We will not be going to Jenin. One can imagine with his wife yet to deliver, Iyad has neither the patience nor attention to broker a solution more satisfactory to both parties. There is no shouting, none of the tantrums that characterized much of my Hollywood experience, but shoulders are tense. During the return to Ramallah, his command of English decimated by disappointment, what the director will allow me is that Iyad feels that given the current climate even the most oblique affiliation between Al Kamandjâti and Freedom Theatre could prove catastrophic even lethal to the music school's project in Jenin. As a filmmaker of curiosity and integrity the director is incandescently frustrated, but as a man of conscience he must also say, 'Who am I to question this? They must live here. We do not.' No, we do not.

Despite vows from various Palestinian officials, the murderers of Juliano Mer-Khamis have not been found. Less than two months after my visit, the Freedom Theatre was stoned by heavily armed Israeli soldiers, members of its staff arrested, the British managing director and the Swedish co-founder of the theatre forced to squat on the ground at gunpoint along with a family of four young children. So who did kill Juliano after all, and how does Al Kamandjâti navigate such treacherous waters? With its eyes most assiduously on its prize.

Shortly after the film crew drops me off at the school's Ramallah compound, Jenin Ensemble violinists Rashed and Najir arrive from that city for a three hour classical rehearsal, as bright-eyed and bushy-tailed as if this was the beginning as opposed to the denouement of a long and arduous day. To my eyes this exemplifies an El Sistema level of commitment among the most enthused of Al Kamandjâti's students, but Ramzi is very quick to differentiate the challenges with which the two institutions are wrestling. In his view the Venezuelans are contending with social problems while functioning as they are under occupation, Al Kamandjâti's problems are primarily political, saying '[entry and transit] permits are not required for concerts in Venezuela.' The nuances here could be argued; and once again I detect a number of resonances here between

Ramzi's project of national cultural identity and that which characterized much of the Black Power movement. Straightforward polemic in both cases deemed a necessity, but its concomitant danger of underestimating the persistence, power and glory of the greys that enhance the nature of man also ever-present. However, returning to my original question of whether the dialectical tension of 'our' music vs. 'their' music that marked my years of 'revolution' is dictating the musical choices, appreciation and development among those with whom I've been spending time, the answer in Al Kamandjâti and Ramzi's philosophy of a musical *intifada* remains a firm, resounding no. Though the vast majority of AK's Music Days performances feature Arabic music, the school's commitment to Western classical music continues.

Classical chamber concerts and their attendant rehearsals have been on-going throughout my week, the participating musicians primarily Kamandjâti instructors and the visiting professionals, the smaller but appreciative audiences a mix of Western expats and the odd older local aficionados. These give teachers a chance to spread their wings for they are musicians first and foremost and such expression is their life's blood. Concerts by the fledgling Ramallah Orchestra in its hometown and Jerusalem form the apex of the Music Days season, and this summer with distinguished French conductor Diego Masson at its helm the offered program will include Beethoven, Mozart and Lebanese composer Marcel Khalife. The son of surrealist painter André Masson, in his youth, during the Algerian war, Diego worked with the Algerian National Liberation Front's underground branch in France and spent two years in French jails for his pains, just one of the reasons he feels a strong and natural solidarity with the Palestinian cause and will likely continue his association with Kamandjâti beyond this initial visit.

I was unaware of the Music Days schedule before planning my travel and was unable to amend my stay to include one of its most potent manifestations of Kamandjâti's musical *intifada*: a concert by its Youth Orchestra inside the processing area of the Qalandia checkpoint.

No permits sought or obtained this time, a bus parked just beyond the surveillance of military cameras, Ramzi, who will be playing viola with band, bidding a small group of older students and staff to vanguard with music stands and large percussion into the area where Palestinians gather before starting the procedure of entry into Israel proper. Having chosen to return to Ben Gurion airport by taxi my previous trip, I myself experienced Qalandia only once during that time. I'd wanted to spend a quick few hours in Jerusalem's Old City and do it in the (far cheaper) Palestinian fashion via Bus 18, which involved passage through steel corridors, gates and bars. There are X-ray machines and bullet-proof glass behind which young soldiers with automatic weapons perused identification papers with expressions that ranged between stoicism and disdain. I'm not a timid person but I became flustered. My hand tangled in the straps of my backpack. It shook. My passport dropped. The young guard asked me why. 'I'm nervous,' I replied. 'I've never done this before.' Which was only the allowable part of that particular truth.

On 23 June 2011 the Kamandjâti musicians still on the bus tune their instruments. When all is prepared those on the bus exit quickly to their places. All but the cellists will perform standing. With the signal given by their resident American conductor Jason Crompton, the twenty-five students and eight teachers of Al Kamandjâti's Youth Orchestra launch into the first movement of Mozart's Sixth Symphony. A crowd of what becomes nearly one hundred gathers as they play, pausing in an oasis of solidarity and joy before the humiliating rite of passage that awaits them just beyond. American author Sandy Tolan, whom I thank for this account, is witness to the event and posts a mobile phone recording on his blog, Ramallah Cafe.

There's no embrace for the music in this environment ringed in steel, but the orchestra's sound is confident and true. The guards take no notice during the Mozart but appear one by one behind the bars during the Bizet, talking amongst themselves and into their radios. The orchestra's performance is without permit and thus illegal, but how illegal? Do they want to arrest children who are playing music, the youngest of whom is nine? They demur. At the concert's end I hear whoops and applause ricocheting about the steel. Back on the bus, the orchestra are exultant, returning to Al Kamandjâti with much singing and playing of tabla and oud. In our Facebook conversation later that evening, my new young cello-playing friend Laila tells me, 'today was my big day. I think music now became part of my life after the concert. We just did something which made us happy.'

'The only way to deal with an unfree world is to become so absolutely free that your very existence is an act of rebellion.' I encounter this quote from Albert Camus and think of Laila and others like her, those she knows and those she doesn't, who are consolidating that free human identity in the compendium of melody, harmony, rhythm, effort and grace that is music.

Taking It Out

14

1954: the purpose of music is 'to remind the listener that he belongs to a certain part of the human race, comes from a certain region, belongs to a certain generation. The music of your place… is a quick and immediate symbol for all the deepest emotions the people of your part of the world share.'

Alan Lomax, ethnomusicologist

December 1985. I am working on a film temporarily located in West Germany's Black Forest. As has become my pattern the film involves some of Hollywood's most esteemed talent in one of their least memorable ventures. It is a few weeks before the Christmas holidays, a quiet time for the modern and spacious sport-oriented hotel in which we are billeted, so quiet and remote among these snow-adorned trees that I am reminded of Stanley Kubrick's The Shining and Jack Nicholson running amok with his axe up and down the corridors of the failing Overlook Hotel. The large leaden pine cones attached to all room keys to discourage their wander add to this impression. They feel like murder weapons. On our second evening, with a later start the next day and with nowhere else to go many of us film folk descend on the hotel's discotheque, which would seem to be 'the' place to be in this small corner of Baden-Württemberg. The disk jockey is a skinny young man in tight white jeans, Flavor Flav oversize shades and a white baseball cap with blinking multi-colored lights. I've a strong suspicion given his jerky movements and wannabe patter that he was once a village stooge, but those days are past. Now he's Mr. Cool.

Up until this moment the records played have been predominantly electro-dynamic EuroPop but this changes without notice to an example of prover-bial German oompah and the floor is suddenly taken by a line of men doing the German slap dance, clothed not in lederhosen but their elegant casual best. I've never witnessed this live before and neither has our American Female Star who has come to stand by my side with her escorts. She is known for her orig-inal approach to fashion is our star, and this evening's ensemble is different textures of cocooning Japanese black with accompanying small, round and pitch dark shades. (I admire her greatly.) As we watch the knees-up, thigh-slapping she murmurs quietly, 'What do you think of this, Candace?' To which I reply, 'I haven't really decided, Diane, but anthropologically it's very interesting.'

March 2005. My blond, blue-eyed, mixed-race nephew has just turned seven. It is his last morning in London before returning to Los Angeles. In the course of one of our last conversations he lifts his arm next to mine and says, 'My skin is white and yours is brown. It doesn't mean anything but it's very, very important.'

April 2010

'…The sun has come

May your light lead us all back to one

Indivisible sum…'

Janelle Monae, '57821'

And what my first thoughts after this meander? That the ambiguities and contentions start with the definition of 'culture'.

Leaving aside the agar gel and Petri dishes of grade-school chemistry classes, culture is listed in the Oxford Dictionary Online as '1. The arts and other manifestations of human intellectual achievement and a refined understanding of this' and '2. The customs, arts, social institutions and achievements of a particular nation, people and other social group'. In the American Webster Online the specificities are reversed with '1. A particular society at a particular time and place' and its corollaries preceding '5. A highly developed state of perfection; having a flawless or impeccable quality' and '11. The state of being cultivated, the result of civilization, enlightenment and discipline acquired by mental and moral training… refinement in taste and manners.' These nuanced reconfigurations more than likely the result of protracted ontological battle between philologists for tradition and purity vs. those for political sensitivity and modernity. The lumbering Third International transported back and forth across oceans since its purchase (and copyright) in 1976 and now but a short step away from my desk also leads with refinement, while Noah Webster's early nineteenth century original, compiled for a predominantly agrarian young America, led with the tilling and preparation of crops. It is this notion of refinement that often produces unrest: what constitutes refinement to whom and by whose standards?

The development of the notion of culture as refined civilization, as promoted and understood by those living in or with the West — with its tensions between the Apollonian high and Dionysian low, the civilized and uncivilized, the questions of which the human ideal, which debased and moving towards sub-human — has been percolating for centuries, but reaches a particular zenith in Europe, splashing into its Northwest Atlantic colonies, during the late-eighteenth and throughout the nineteenth centuries. It is during this era, with European global imperialism at its height, that much of Western classical music's 'core repertoire' is composed. This is not to suggest that the giants of said repertoire composed with imperialist imperatives in mind; quite the opposite in fact in the case of Mozart, Beethoven and Verdi, to name but three. Indeed the reduction of their Promethean struggles against autocracy and complacency to luxury entertainments is at the very least lazy and deeply irreverent; but in their vast majority, composers of the period were dependent on some form of patronage to keep body and soul together. Their continuing upkeep, let alone success, was often dependent upon how well they pleased their ruling class masters and very much involved gifting said masters with works that soothed, titillated and/or reflected well upon themselves. Mozart's end in a pauper's grave is sober testament to what refusal or simply the artistic inability to conform to this imperative might bring. And so this music becomes the music of the 'cultured' just as 'cultured' becomes what this dominant group believes itself to be.

Beyond this self-important and self-protective group, the so-called common people continued, unperturbed, with their own forms of expression: music, often still as in earlier times, extemporaneous accompaniment to the percussions of axe or sledge hammer, the slap of dough on a table or wet laundry on a rock, the rhythm of a brush on said laundry accompanied by birdsong and the rush or ripple of the water developed in scant leisure into plaintive stories and rollicking reels, most often by those excused or unfit for physical labor for reasons of genius, age or infirmity.

Those who have the time and wont to form hierarchies do so, generally placing their own preferences at the top of any scale with the 'particular society' definition of culture generally glazed with the veneer of anthropology, often stinking of condescension. Case in point myself in the *Schwarzwald*, where I was pleased to identify the knee-slapping Germans as 'tribal', divining no commonality of group self-expression between them and a room of happily partying African-Americans joining together for an Electric Slide. I thus became guilty of the hypocrisy I decried: thinking, and often declaring, oneself impartial in the analysis of an Other while being riddled by the presumptions, if not downright prejudices, of one's class, race, religion, nation… Hardly laudatory behavior, but not problematic so long as those classified as inferior are unaware of their designated status. However, when via education and/or infiltration the 'lower' become aware of their footing in the eyes and power structures of the 'higher' things begin to get more complex.

In the twentieth century as the empires of past centuries

began to collapse, as education became more available and infiltrations increased, this awareness became more widespread. We Lowers — despite the *Schwarzwald*-displayed arrogance, my identification has generally remained with the Lowers which given where I've been and how I've lived could be construed by others as a reach, if not outright dishonesty; but again I say, we Lowers, entered the rooms that had been previously closed to us. We became aware of and then penetrated discussions, often aghast at the lazy and gratuitously cruel language in which arguments were presented, our rhetorical guns often blazing. In the more rarefied halls of academic dialectic our passion was often categorized as unseemly and overly personalized.

These arguments weren't personal, we were told, rather the stuff of Cartesian discourse, the balance and harmony of Apollo as ever rather than the chthonic abandon of Dionysus. Feigning the delicately harmonious pose is rather more difficult, however, in fact downright counter-intuitive when it's your head, your heart and soul receiving the blows. The 'This isn't personal; it's business' trope of countless gangster movies raises its head. For how different the structures of criticism deeming the protestations of Lowers unreasonable and unseemly, to the line of poor bastards snuffed out or criminally intimidated in the Godfathers' preservation of their statuses quo? Which is not to ignore, though many of us did, that the 'Uppers' were/are human as well. Demonization was often part of the process, something to be counteracted with hindsight and maturity if not before but not always achieved by either 'us' or 'them'. The wages of cultural war…

'Not [that impossible twaddle], Lewis! I'm talking about Music!'
John Thaw as Inspector Morse in an episode the title of which
I couldn't trace but applicable to almost any of their number.

The above, of course, not just the domain of the redoubtable Morse, but why this territorial and restrictive definition of music? Why the arrogance that all non-Western art music is ephemeral vulgarity? Why is it a 'given' that the sentimentalisms of 'Die Schöne Müllerin' or fourteenth century French troubadours are more artistic than that of Motown's Smoky Robinson or Oscar Hammerstein II? Why is Schiller's lyric poetry categorically more compelling than that of Stevie Wonder or Joni Mitchell? How different the harmonies of urban adolescent doo-wop from those of Pretorius, Palestrina and Hildegard of Bingen? Or from the opposite stance, how can the music of Schubert be deemed less viscerally soulful than Aretha Franklin's gospel rendition of 'Holy, Holy'? Why is this critical horse race even necessary? So much of it about and permeated with power and the various dances of its manifestation be they minuet, sabre or the Broadway bugaloo. The preservation of old hegemonies countered by the defiant establishment of new, and on and on, until consequently in the area of 'refined' culture, its definition and defence, battle lines became more and more entrenched at every boundary of the divisions, and woe betide the independent thinker who strayed from his or her patch. One can wonder if there shouldn't be as many words for music as there are Sami words for snow — as opposed to Inuit for which contrary to urban myth there really aren't that many; for beyond this all contention a basic truism remains: that homo sapiens possess this particular affinity for the progressions of pitched sounds, scientifically established, common throughout our species, this miracle we simply call music (*or moosiqa or ongaku or gAN or glazba…*). It is one of our basic glories; so why so hard to relax and celebrate the shared aspects of the wonder, especially as the need for its balm becomes ever more desperate?

In 1943 celebrated conductor Leopold Stokowski published

Music for All of Us, a book curious for its time and certainly for one of his rarefied profession. In it he declared 'to say certain music is good and other bad is an attempt at mental and spiritual dictatorship... Freedom of thought about music and reaction to music are indispensable to true culture... The difference of reaction to music and all art is fundamental and eternal.' The difference between Stokowski and prominent contemporary colleagues such as Toscanini and Walter Damrosch and their definitions of 'real music' could not have been more stark. Described by historian Joseph Horowitz as 'an epicure, a sensualist, a relativist and an experimentalist' by this time in his career Stokowski had finessed the sounds of the Cincinnati and more prominently the Philadelphia Orchestras, introduced countless contemporary works including those by Schoenberg, Stravinsky, Varese, Berg, Webern, Szymanowski and Copland to American audiences, had appeared in Walt Disney's Fantasia famously shaking hands with Mickey Mouse and in One Hundred Men and a Girl with a post-pubescent Deanna Durbin.

Unlike Adorno and befitting one who was a Music Director of the NBC Symphony Orchestra, Stokowski celebrated the possibilities of broadcasted music, extolling its extension beyond the privilege of the favored few and into the expanses of nature, declaring radio 'one of the greatest mechanical means toward the evolution of Mind and Spirit.' Eccentric with his orchestral seatings and his transcriptions of Bach, Mussorgsky and Wagner among others, flamboyant and often cursory in his professional and amoral in his private life, Stokowski was both lionized and vilified during his lifetime and contemporary attitudes towards him are often bemused. Easy then for a book such as *Music for All of Us* to be ignored. Such books are almost never publishing successes and in retrospect can seem little more than vanity projects. *Music for All of Us* is often not even cited in biographical accounts of Stokowski including a dedicated website stokowski.org; but in its protean curiosity and recognition of the dignity and worth of non-Western and non-art music, its championship of non-intellectual and thereby democratic appreciation of all music, it is a beacon for the challenges of our times.

How exemplary the under-noticed wisdom of Leopold Stokowski as notions of refined culture continue to be dominated by hierarchies: what is best, what is middling, what is beneath contempt; as well as the seemingly inevitable consequence that in the face of cultural hierarchy defiant and defensive cultural (in its anthropological sense) tribalism has been the natural response. As earlier mentioned this defiant defensiveness was a default position for the politically aware of my baby-boomer generation, particularly those members of despised minorities. We fought hard, winning as many battles as we lost, many of us thinking ourselves forever young, forever counter-establishment while believing that our discovered and constructed new truths would stand forever. Ignoring history, both what had passed before and that which was rushing towards us, as well as the fact that ours was not the only reality, many of us slipped unconsciously but relentlessly into conservatism, anathema to our credo and yet all too obvious evidence of this truism abounds. Here but one:

In African-American political discourse during the earlier stages of Barack Obama's 2008 presidential campaign, there was among many leaders a strenuous reluctance to accept Obama's non-civil rights movement credentials. For months a philosophical wrestle with the notion of the first generation's Moses — those who had sat-in, marched and ridden in the face of often violent opposition — making room for, let alone giving way to the next generation Joshua was a major preoccupation. *From Webster's Third International: conservatism (n.) '... the ten-*

dency to accept an existing fact, order, situation or phenomenon… strong resistance to innovation, relative freedom from change…' Many of the Moses generation were emotionally, philosophically and even economically invested in a late twentieth-century definition of African-American identity and righteous political behavior and did not want to budge let alone evolve away from its ground zero. Had not this definition of identity and commitment served us well, effected real change? Why move? What price such a move? How can we be different from what we've believed ourselves to be? And in the same moment, how dare anyone accuse us of conservatism! How can freedom-fighters ever be labeled conservative?

In the face of a democratization and refiguring of hoary taxonomies in a variety of areas including cultural 'refinement' that we baby-boomers achieved, one might hope for a reduction of combativeness, a reallocation of energy, but instead many of us remain in a defensive crouch. In the words of fellow baby-boomer Amin Maalouf, we are often 'entrenching [ourselves] in a state of permanent emergency… clinging to tribalism for lack of imagination' while so much that might enrich our lives and that of those around us is dismissed or just missed.

I embarked on this exploration out of a combination of curiosity about how the young people involved in these orchestras saw themselves and 'their' music in relation to their salutary adoption of the Western classics and concern that our/my/their music was being subsumed in the transaction. I felt the concern because I was a veteran of cultural wars and because I'd penetrated at least the edges of classical music's inner sanctum and thus become aware of the ideas and behavior patterns of a certain portion of its acolytes. Which is not to say that I've eschewed its many pleasures. It was and remains a seductive place, one where losing perspective of its importance is all too easy.

In the world beyond intellectual battles over cultural hierarchies, the music of salvation, that which soothes the soul and/or galvanizes it to revolutionary action is far more often the music of, by and for the common people, the folks outside the sanctuaries with little time and less attention for the intellectual exercises performed in their names. Even as my own tastes were expanding, even as I reveled in the glories of Western classical music, I was most protective of African-American music, 'my' music, because of the attitudes I encountered within intellectual and musical sanctums. Many of them were historical rather than contemporary, but maintaining objective focus when encountering words like coon and nigger alongside determinations of childishness and naïveté in so-called critical discourse is more than challenging. At times my annoyance obscured the reality that, by virtue of their own power and contemporary media, 'our' beats and the transformative forces of 'our' jazz and 'our' street musics are globally ubiquitous. They have fired and continue to fire liberations personal, communal and political; and perhaps the continual linkage of jazz to the dark side and criminality is emblematic of societal fears of its potency and our potency as well. To whit, I found myself a ragged and vaguely sheepish exemplar of the combative baby boomer default position that continues to exercise huge influence in arts policy and academe even as our children feel their ways towards other possibilities.

Throughout my unscientific wanderings, in addition to perceiving that those in extremis were loath to discriminate when it came to the sources of joy, I found continual serendipities in more comfortable environs: that for those serious about music, in either the listening or the producing below the age of thirty-five, boundaries, categories, arbitrary exclusions were unimportant, ignored and often pointedly upended. The technological revolution has been a major influence of course: the ability to access and disseminate different styles and genres at mind-boggling speeds, to explore, sample and combine, to find like-minded co-conspirators either in a bordering street or halfway across the world without the mediation of older authorities and orthodoxies. Parents, copyright holders and political states do their best to regulate both the rush and the information but with decreasing success, and so the young formulate their own tastes. Musicians trained in different genres exchange and combine their talents according to their affinities, with sincerity and the necessary level of expertise being the only prerequisites. The physical transport of bodies to another place is far easier than once was but, with the rise of additional technologies, no longer essential even for live collaboration. However, beyond their comfortable interface with galloping technology and diverse cultural expressions, it can also be surmised that the younger have taken many of the hard-won realignments from former decades as a given, this thinking in music being reinforced by a widening of approach at a number of elite conservatories.

In 1985, exasperated by the rarefied, ivory tower attitudes rampant in his field, as well as the failure of many conservatories to prepare their students for the realities of both a world and a profession unable to accommodate insular, self-absorbed elite graduates in their thousands year upon year, music professor Peter Renshaw established the Connect program at London's Guildhall School. The Connect program sent students and teachers into surrounding often stressed communities to engage and inspire young people through musical creativity in all genres. In so doing the skills of its own students were honed beyond performance into teaching, composition and community leadership. With the century's turn the Scottish Academy of Music inaugurated its Musicworks program dedi-

cated to bringing music to underserved communities throughout Scotland, and Juilliard President Joseph Polisi amended
that school's orientation by including the notion of the artist as
citizen in both curriculum and practice. Once a bastion of elite
insularity, Juilliard now actively encourages its students to take
pro-active roles in promoting the arts through embracing leadership and example in all kinds of communities, counseling
that there is no dividing line between excellence and social consciousness. Despite the hiccup at the beginning of 2011 generated by anxieties as to whether the socially transfiguring mission of El Sistema is compatible with that of enabling elite
musicians towards their callings, the New England
Conservatory maintained a continuing relationship with
Fundamusical, with at this writing the third of at least five
classes of Abreu — now called Sistema — Fellows being prepared to establish nucleos north of Venezuela. Its fellow
Boston institution the Berklee College of Music includes in its
mission statement 'to encourage our students to appreciate and
apply music's enormous force for the enrichment of society
and intercultural understanding.' At this point, these efforts
even collectively have nowhere near the scope of
Fundamusical. The student/participants are comparatively
small in number, but they are multiplying; and in their ever-
widening spheres of influence we can wish for effects akin to
chaos theory's butterfly wings. We can wish and we can work
towards an ideal of humanity with mutual respect and without
borders, but we also cannot be unaware of the forces assembled against this ideal.

Beyond the obvious political contretemps of states and ethnicities, the older members of which are dedicated to annihila-
tion of the Other for miscellaneous spoils of war and for
which enhanced cultural differences are an effective and canny
tool, many in the commercial cultural industries still earn their

gilded crust via an emphasis on difference. To the cultural corporate conglomerates 'our' music vs. 'their' music, the usses and thems, are of no vested interest whatsoever aside from the ability of both to propagate more coin; but its subliminal impact can be particularly effective among the less educated, travelled and secure.

Stamford, CT. 2009. I am playing with the notion of what relation karaoke might have to the soul and visiting a local sports bar over the Thanksgiving holiday. The bar is named for and owned by the one star athlete of my high school years who went on to excel in Major League Baseball. I'm thinking to ruminate on various roads taken as well de-construct my first encounter with karaoke; but I am dissuaded by a recent incident in which six local young African-American women repeatedly punched, kicked and pulled the hair of a slightly older Latina from Westchester. Said Latina had displeased them with her rendition A Dios Le Pido by Colombian pop superstar Juanes. Bouncers ejected the six from the bar and the manager called the police who picked them up walking down the boulevard. Upon their arrest one of them is quoted as saying 'The bouncers told us to leave. We couldn't perform our song.'

News reports on the incident did not reference the obvious racial and class differences between the protagonists. The Latina was demurely attractive and driven to the evening by her husband who later wondered 'I don't know why they're here.' The black girls were found walking in a community where cars are de rigueur. Their mug shots show them wearing cheap clothes and the amateurishly attached store-bought hair extensions that declare that no one has urged them towards the innate beauty in themselves. No mention is made of drink. They simply wanted to perform their song. They needed the release and the mille-second of X Factor limelight attendant to performing their song because how many other opportunities for respect however cursory did they get in their lives? Their song made them feel special and free. Why was this Spanish girl taking up their time and their space and not even singing in English? There are too many damn spics in this town these days and we were here first...

*Us vs. Them among the young and dispossessed in the twenty-first centu-
ry and not to be ignored. I chose not to go to Bobby Valentine's that holiday.
The liquor would be flowing even more freely than usual with all the college
students home celebrating their potency and youth and I, possibly with ignorant arrogance, had already rushed to my karaoke conclusion. As it was neither my taste nor my need, I'd turned my back.*

In comfort and sophisticated diversity one can lose touch with
the core to which Alan Lomax refers in his definition of music,
'sound like evocative scents and sights, that are reminders of
belonging to, and treasuring something more particular, home'.
For me that included the easy sway of Motown at its peak, the
drape of a jazz musician's jacket, the shimmering sleek of a
vocalist's sheath dress in club light. We all need stories, and
crave stories about ourselves.

*I see the Alvin Ailey dance company for the first time in many years. I
haven't gone expressly for their signature masterpiece Revelations because I
have seen it and seen it, the first time some forty years previously in a
Cambridge, Massachusetts high school auditorium; and I am beyond any need
of seeing it again. I admire the new work, reveling in the eloquently moving
and muscled brown bodies, their beauty and their skill. This is a good thing,
I think, the Company needs to move with the times, keep Black at least on
the near edge of the avant-garde. I'd been fearing artistic complacency; but with
the first notes of Revelations I am undone, plunged into a warm sea of who
I am and who I was, the notes and the images accompanying them nereids, dol-
phins swirling about me, shoring me up. I live away from that which raised me
and I was wrong. I am a cosmopolitan exponent of humanity without borders, artistic expression mitigating difference, but I needed this reminder. I
emerge from the theatre stronger than when I went in, fortified by cultural traditions intrinsically entwined with my race/memory, reinforced in who I am.*

This call for exchange and cross-pollination is not a desire
for homogeneity, which is already well-represented in the proliferation of grandstanding but soulless pop. Variegated tex-

tures make for both interest and strength, tapestry with natural fibers being the ideal; the color and integrity of each thread essential to the whole, rather than that akin to sheets of polyvinyl chloride. Nor does this call ignore the challenge of the appearance, let alone the reality, of fairness for public funding/policy bodies in multi-cultural societies plagued by mutual suspicions and self-interests, both enlightened and its opposite. With no desire to tar more than a few of such dealings with the brush of cupidity, there is often money as well as respect and pride involved in recognition of this group's artistic expression vs. that one's — and those whose feelings of power and self-worth are invested in how much we get for our program as opposed to theirs.

This is not to say that the time for vigilance is over; most multi-cultural nations are far from post-racial societies. One need look no further than the constant attempts to humiliate and delegitimize the presidency of Barack Obama with suspicions as to his birth and academic prowess, pictures of him as a chimpanzee, his being referred to as tar baby, a dick and a crack addict, racially signifying and explosive terms meant to pass as acceptable political discourse. And then there is such as the Tea Party demand to the state legislature of Tennessee that 'no portrayal of minority experience in history which actually occurred shall obscure the experience of the Founding Fathers or the majority of citizens including those who reached positions of leadership' shall appear in the history books utilized in state school — i.e., let's not mention slavery (let alone slave progeny) and three-fifths of a man: the original Constitutional designation of how slaves should be counted in census — or the treatment of Native Americans or the internment of the Japanese or the demonization of Muslims. In other words, let us raise our children in self-congratulating ignorance. Such initiatives are in service to forces unable to accept fundamental humanistic change, and one can never be guilty of or allow complacency when confronted with the threat to human decency — let alone progress — that they pose. Lessons must be reinforced and conflicts revisited for their educational value, but to continually re-fight the same battles in a world of burgeoning population and diminishing resources smacks of the suicidal. This is not to say that abandoning such battles is easy or even natural. They have gone on so long, and are also so much a part of the human tragi-comedy.

For veterans of twentieth century culture wars, conflict can possess the comfort of broken-in shoes and familiar refrains; and absorbing a new music, like absorbing a new language is often far more challenging with age. With the young and itching for battle, as unmindful of history as we were ourselves, I sometimes find myself discerning desires to re-invent the wheel but, as in so many other respects, without the twentieth century's luxurious perception of infinite possibilities. So perhaps what we might consider now is a harkening back to the agrarian definition of culture, the tilling and preparation of a soil to maximize an outcome of quality capable of nourishing a needful population which, with ever more limited resources and space, necessitates that each plot sustain more than one entity. In this tradition one crop is not allowed to overwhelm its cohabitants and while species' purities are preserved, inevitable hybrids that are improvements and/or delights become a welcome part of the harvest.

And in the midst of all the innovative adaptations of thinking, policy and practice, not losing sight of the art and phenomenon that is music's simplest origins and appeals: its connection to the deepest fundaments of what humans are, need and dream of.

15

Codas…

In the decades following our years of political and cultural reorientation the music scene of my alma mater has been transformed. Though its emphasis on Western classical music remains, the Harvard Music Department now offers courses in Cross-Cultural Perspectives, Jazz Harmony and South Indian Music. There is an Ethnomusicology Lab and a college Jazz Band and the spiritual-oriented Kuumba Singers. The Quincy Jones Professor of African-American Music is a white female trumpet-playing ethnomusicologist who specializes in jazz and was a founding member of the Boston area's Klezmer Conservatory Band. Classical stars among Harvard alumni John Adams, William Christie and Yo Yo Ma have been joined by jazz virtuosi Joshua Redman and Don Braden, and among the university's African-American PhDs are baroque opera specialist Harris Saunders and nineteenth century Italian opera specialist Naomi André. 'Our' music vs. 'their' music no longer. Choice. The twenty-first century.

I attend an Esperanza Spalding concert soon after she has won the 2011 Grammy Award for Best New Artist. A bassist and vocalist, she is the first jazz musician to do so. She is precocious. Before the age of eight she had taught herself to play the violin well enough to join a local chamber society of which she remained a member until she was fifteen. She is beautiful, light-complected with a nimbus of Afro-styled hair. In the twentieth-century, by dint of the one-drop rule, she would have been categorized as black, but now she has a choice and describes herself as from a 'multi-lingual' household, her mother Welsh, Hispanic and Native American, her absent father black. At times she and her brother slept on the floor to avoid becoming collateral damage of gunfire in her Portland, Oregon neighborhood.

She is said to be tall but her pliant slender form looks fragile next to the bass, her only concession to wardrobe diktats for female musical performance her gracefully muscled naked arms. Her fingers appear as delicate as her vocal lines; but they are not, as she is not, as she grabs a freedom that wasn't available to performers of my generation. There's a winsomeness about her, about her music. Even when it is pensive she and it are all joy and possibilities and already achieved realities. She embodies what we hoped for. I feel grateful for her and to her and very glad.

When the Venezuelans return to the site of their 2007 triumph in London's Royal Albert Hall in August 2011, the word Youth no longer figures in their name. Many of their members are still in their late teens and the average age still but twenty-four; however, with a nod to their burgeoning experience and expertise they are now simply the Simon Bolivar Symphony Orchestra with Gustavo Dudamel on the podium for a program consisting only of Mahler's Second Symphony. Gustavo remains the supreme star in Fundamusical's firmament but he is not alone. In July 2011, twenty-six year-old Diego Matheuz was named Principal Conductor of Venice's La Fenice opera house, while conductors Christian Vasquez and Manuel Lopez are finding their own distinction in numerous international venues. The atmosphere in the hall was attentive and celebratory but no manner of stomping applause could coax the orchestra to violate the resurrection spell with the frolic of Latin encores. The orchestra bowed, smiled and left. They were near the end of a three week tour, flying out to Istanbul the following morning. No mambo then. No salsa party in the green rooms. Professional, seasoned musicians, happy in their work, but taking care of business and thereby heralding another milestone in the development of Fundamusical.

Mere hours after the Venezuelans depart, street violence erupts in a northern borough of London, when a peaceful demonstration to obtain answers from the police in regards to the death of a young black man in custody, is wrested from the intentions of family and friends of the deceased and mutates into days and nights of wanton looting, arson, intimidation and even murder of non-participating citizens obstructive to the progress of marauding perpetrators.

Dispatched to various locations in first London and then other cities by many of the same social networking techniques used by organizers of the liberation movements in Tunisia, Egypt, Bahrain and Syria, a good number — but by no means all — young, a good number — but by no means all — of color, and a good number — but by no means all — economically powerless participants directed their efforts toward the acquisition of stuff, as in 'head to Oxford Circus pure terror and havoc & free stuff' and 'we're not broke but who says no to free stuff?' These were not bread riots or runs on supermarkets as happened during onslaught and aftermath of Hurricane Katrina in New Orleans. The free stuff in question was not the necessities of life but the accoutrements of lifestyles: mobile telephones, flat-screen televisions, bicycles, street fashion and trainers. Though there had been warnings about youth unemployment and disenfranchisement bubbling up from the streets for months, the four afternoons and nights of seemingly amoral and wanton destruction caught almost all corners of Britain unawares and stupefied.

Much is and will continue to be discussed as to the whys and wherefores. For the left the first accused are the swinging cuts to youth services with no regard to consequence by a Conservative-led government bent on balancing the budget at all costs; for the right, a breakdown in parenting and senses of personal responsibility. But so terrifyingly vivid a *cri de coeur* suggests also that custodial educations combined with the collapse of family structures and the insights of reasonable religion have created a population with no knowledge of expressions of self-worth beyond accessorizing consumerism. If I have this, if I wear this, I am styled. I am Somebody. If said accessories cum-necessities are impossible to obtain via education and jobs, then who can honestly say that I/we shouldn't go after them by any means necessary? Why should we believe otherwise when all of society and culture, everything we see is dominated by fat cats, politicians and bankers, celebrities of all kinds with gangster-ish appetites for bling of all kinds? When this entire economy is built on consumption, you telling me I can't have my share? It was thrilling to be part of something beyond myself that moved and did something beyond just me, that was bigger than just me. And you treat us like dirt…

With little if any import given to that which money can't buy, in a cultural where identity is dominated not by race or religion or anything intrinsically human, is dominated by hard cash and stuff, how can we who are franchised be shocked when with the right/wrong kind of pressure a societal gasket blows and an angry percentage of our populace, seeking the only agency they know, rushes for the gold? As we dig deep searching for answers and wonder if we can afford not to invest in solutions, the contrast between the rampaging, rapacious lost souls of August 2011 — music often crashing about them but seldom coming from within — and the hundreds of thousands served, even saved, via music in Venezuela could not be more stark. Lessons to be learned.

Diminuendo con Amore

At a small theatre in lower Manhattan I attend *A Boy and His Soul*, an autobiographical one-man show by African-American performer Colman Domingo chronicling his 1970s and 80s West Philadelphia working-class upbringing, for which soul music was far more than background music; it was often the conduit through which his family members communicated with one another. It was also the medium through which he found himself. For decades I've been convinced that I've left this music behind, that it wasn't speaking to who I'd become, wasn't pure enough or edgy enough, but I am warmed by the associations, laughing with and testifying to the race memories and humbled by one scene in particular.

On a sticky summer night, Jay and Edie, his hard-working mother, are sitting outside on the porch when Aretha Franklin's ethereal version of *Daydreaming* starts playing on the radio. In the wash of Aretha's near conversational artistry, Edie's cares from poverty, her worry and sadness just melt away. She is 'regal in the light of the new moon' as she opens her imitation leather pocketbook and her nine year-old son's hands to the sky and the ethereal counsel and possibilities of 'Ree Ree's' song.

'O Sweetheart just hold open your hands! Let God see that you are open to change… Just because you wish for it don't mean it won't come true!' My heart stretches wide to embrace Edie and her complete appreciation of all Ree Ree's song had to give her. I am with her in the light of the new moon.

Not long after, I attend a riveting performance of Mahler 1 conducted by Gustavo Dudamel. I am overtaken by the energy and exultant joy of the occasion, the originality of his interpretation. My blood is fizzing, but Edie has not been displaced in my heart. She and Mahler are dancing together, with Malian kora virtuoso Toumani Diabate and Duke Ellington, the subtle phrasing of Fred Astaire and the unicorn's peals of Finnish composer Kaija Saariaho.

Music has its own imperatives, beyond all discussion.

As Colman concludes, 'It's called Soul Music. It gets into your body, and it takes you.'

Acknowledgments

My thanks first and foremost to Martin Campbell-White, dear friend and joint Chief Executive of Askonas Holt Ltd for opening doors to the Barenboim-Said Foundation and Fundamusical thereby turning wishes into horses.

To Christina Bartsch of the Barenboim-Said Foundation Berlin for organizing my interviews with Ramzi Aburedwan, Rawan Kurdi and Karim Said and to Muna Khleifi of Barenboim-Said Ramallah for the contribution of her time and perspectives on the West Bank.

To Dr José Antonio Abreu for his generous invitation to Caracas and the hospitality of Fundamusical, to Bolivia Bottome for her gracious and informative guidance during my time there; to Gloria Carnevali, currently writing a comprehensive history of Fundamusical and the El Sistema movement for sharing of hard-won information on El Sistema's early years; and to José Alberto Rivas for insights into Venezuelan character and the country's recent history.

To Sergio Mims for the pre-distribution copy of Kinshasa Symphony, which I first learned of on his black film blog Shadow and Act, and Anne Shreffler, Chair of Harvard's Music Department for an overview of that institution's more recent demographic.

I spoke to many, many during the course of this ponder, but I'd like to thank in particular, Dr Richard Holloway, Sean Gregory, Director of Creative Learning at the Barbican Centre and Guildhall School, with special mentions to Suzanne Lynn for her sympathetic devil's advocacy and Peter Sellars for his vigorous shaking of my shoulders and the example of his New Crowned Hope.

And finally, my thanks to Martin Rynja for his patience, suggestions and faith in so idiosyncratic a project and his team at Gibson Square for their intelligent and rigorous wrangles with my text. I often stubbornly resisted but was improved by every turn; and to Jamie Bernstein, whose special talent for detail came as an eleventh hour gift.

Further Reading

Adorno, Theodor W., *Essays on Music*, Richard Leppert (ed.), University of California Press, London, 2002

Barenboim, Daniel, *Everything is Connected*, Weidenfeld & Nicolson, London, 2008

Barenboim, Daniel and Edward W. Said, *Parallels and Paradoxes*, edited by Ara Guzelimian, Bloomsbury, London, 2003

Barghouti, Mourid, *I Saw Ramallah*, Ahdaf Soueif (trans.) Bloomsbury, London, 2004

Bindman, David and Henry Louis Gates, Jr. (ed.) *The Image of the Black in Western Art*, Volume 3 Part 1, Belknap Press of Harvard University Press, London, 2010

Booth, Eric, 'El Sistema's Open Secrets', paper delivered at the League of American Orchestras, National Symposium on the El Sistema Movement in the U.S., May 2010

Cheah, Elena, *An Orchestra Beyond Borders*, Verso, London, 2009

Darwish, Mahmoud, *The Butterfly's Burden*, Fady Joudah (trans.) Bloodaxe Books, Tarset, Northumberland, 2007

DeBoeck Filip & Marie-Françoise Plissart, *Kinshasa Tales of the Invisible City*, Ludion, Brussels, 2004

Domingo, Colman, *A Boy and His Soul*, 2009

Douglas, Ann, *Terrible Honesty Mongrel Manhattan in the 1920s*, Farrar, Straus and Giroux, New York, 1995

Ehrenreich, Barbara, *Dancing in the Streets A History of Collective Joy*, Granta Books, London, 2007

Figes, Orlando, *Natasha's Dance*, Allen Lane The Penguin Press, London, 2002

George, Nelson, *The Death of Rhythm and Blues*, Pantheon Books, New York, 1988

Gillett, Charlie, *The Sound of the City*, Outerbridge & Dienstfrey, New York, 1970

Horowitz, Joseph, *Artists in Exile*, Harper Perennial, New York, 2008

Horowitz, Joseph, *Classical Music in America*, W.W. Norton & Co., London, 2007

Lehman, David, *A Fine Romance Jewish Songwriters*, American Songs, Schocken, New York, 2009

Levitan, Daniel, *This is Your Brain on Music*, Dutton, New York, 2006

Maalouf, Amin, *On Identity*, Barbara Bray (trans), The Harvill Press, London, 2000

Polisi, Joseph W., *The Artist as Citizen*, Amadeus Press, Pompton Plains, NJ, 2005

Ross, Alex, *The Rest is Noise*, Farrar Straus and Giroux, New York, 2007

Sondheim, Stephen, *Finishing the Hat* Volume 1, Ebury Press, London, 2010

Stokowski, Leopold, *Music for All of Us*, Simon & Schuster, New York, 1943

Tolan, Sandy, 'Operation Mozart', Ramallah Café.com, 25 June 2011

Wichert, Rachel Nussbaum, 'Emotion and Zeitoper in the Weimar Era', *Music and Emotions*, Collegium, Helsinki, 2010